Cars of the '50s

Mike Mueller

MBI Publishing
Company

This edition published in 2002 by MBI Publishing Company, Galtier Plaza, Suite 200, 380 Jackson Street, St. Paul, MN 55101-3885 USA

The information in this book is true and complete to the best of our knowledge. All recommendations are made without any guarantee on the part of the author or Publisher, who also disclaim any liability incurred in connection with the use of this data or specific details.

We recognize that some words, model names and designations, for example, mentioned herein are the property of the trademark holder. We use them for identification purposes only. This is not an official publication.

MBI Publishing Company books are also available at discounts in bulk quantity for industrial or sales-promotional use. For details write to Special Sales Manager at Motorbooks International Wholesalers & Distributors, Galtier Plaza, Suite 200, 380 Jackson Street, St. Paul, MN 55101-3885 USA.

Library of Congress Cataloging-in-Publication Data Available

ISBN 0-7603-1381-4

Printed in China

Contents

Acknowledgments

Creating this short-winded epic wouldn't have been at all possible without the patience, cooperation, and, above all, hospitality of the many proud car collectors whose classic fifties machines appear on these pages. Although the author would love to thank each and every one personally, he is well aware that listing their names here would require far less effort. But seriously, thanks so much everyone for your kindness. In basic order of appearance, the lucky owners are:

Larry Young, Port Charlotte, Florida, 1955, 1956, and 1957 Chevrolets; Bob Dykstra, Ageless Autos, Zeeland, Michigan, 1950 Ford; Gerald Schantz, Ormond Beach, Florida, 1957 Cadillac Eldorado Brougham; Bill and Barbara Jacobsen, Silver Dollar Classic Cars, Odessa, Florida, 1959 Chevrolet Impala; Jim and Betty Pardo, Naples, Florida, 1951 Buick Special; Larry Young, Port Charlotte, Florida, 1955 Chevrolet Bel Air convertible; Wilton and Terry Davis, Valrico, Florida, 1955 Ford Victoria; Ronald Layton, Sparta, New Jersey, 1955 Mercury Montclair Sun Valley; Mike Bloore, Lutz, Florida, 1957 Ford Skyliner Retractable; Don and Pat Petrus, Winter Haven, Florida, 1957 Ford Thunderbird; Walter and Marion Gutowski, Lakeland, Florida, 1958 Buick Limited convertible; Bill Henefelt, Clearwater, Florida, 1959 Cadillac Series 62 convertible; Charles and Virginia Stoneking, Winter Haven, Florida, 1959 Edsel Ranger; Art and June Ubbens, Lake Wales, Florida, 1955 Plymouth Belvedere; Robert and Mary McVeigh, Lake Park, Florida, 1959 Pontiac Catalina convertible; John Young, Mulberry, Florida, 1954 Corvette; Edwin Hobart, Naples, Florida, 1954 Kaiser Darrin; Rich Miller, Clearwater, Florida, 1957 Chevrolet Bel Air convertible; George Shelley, Pompano Beach, Florida, 1957 Chrysler 300C; Floyd Garrett, Fernandina Beach, Florida, 1957 Ford Fairlane; Don McCullen, Gainesville, Florida, 1957 Studebaker Golden Hawk; Marvin and Joan Hughes, Ocala, Florida, 1957 Dodge Coronet D500 convertible; Gary Ogeltree, Fayetteville, Georgia, 1958 Plymouth Fury; Doug West, Preston, Idaho, 1959 DeSoto Adventurer; Era Harvey, Leesburg, Florida, 1950 Skorpion, 1951

Crosley, and 1958 King Midget; Gene Schild, Des Plaines, Illinois, 1953 Packard Caribbean; Rick Lay, Athens, Tennessee, 1953 Kaiser Dragon; Dave Horton, Lakeland, Florida, 1954 Willys Aero Lark; Harry Fry, Lake Wales, Florida, 1951 Crosley Farm-O-Road; George and Katherine Baumann, Davie, Florida, 1954 Hudson Hornet; Marc Harr, Ormond Beach, Florida, 1955 Packard Clipper; Larry and Vickie Gehm, Melbourne, Florida, 1954 Ford Customline Ranch Wagon; Erol and Susan Tuzcu, Del Ray Beach, Florida, 1957 Chevrolet Nomad; Al Whitcombe, Ambler, Pennsylvania, 1956 Ford F100 pickup; Halderman Ford, Kutztown, Pennsylvania, 1991 Ford F150 XLT 4x4; Bob and Linda Ogle, Champaign, Illinois, 1956 Chevrolet Cameo Carrier pickup; Bob and Debbie Higgins, Davie, Florida, 1957 Chevrolet 3100 pickup; Dan Topping, Tifton, Georgia, 1957 Dodge Sweptside D100 pickup; Ron Fisher, Indianapolis, Indiana, 1957 Ford Ranchero; Doug Stapleton, Bradenton, Florida, 1959 Chevrolet El Camino; Stuart Echolls, Lakeland, Florida, 1955 Dodge Royal; James Wienke, Homer, Illinois, 1955 Ford Crown Victoria; Dan Newcombe of Golden Classics, Safety Harbor, Florida, 1958 Dodge Coronet; Dwight and Mabel Caler, Bradenton, Florida, 1950 Studebaker Champion; William Stead, Lake Mary, Florida, 1953 Henry J; and Gene Jr., Sherri, and Christie DeBlasio, Plantation Florida, 1955 Chevrolet Nomad.

Introduction

The Decade That Just Keeps Rolling On

For many among us it was the longest ten years in history, recorded or otherwise. By definition it was simply another decade, one that began on January 1, 1950, then ended on December 31, 1959. Or did it? Just as time marches on, so too have the fifties, those Fabulous Fifties, right on through the sixties, seventies, eighties, and into the nineties. Sure, memories tend to linger—they wouldn't be memories if they didn't. But for whatever reasons, remembrances of the fifties have not only refused to fade from the American consciousness, they have, in many cases, grown larger than life at a rate unmatched by virtually any other time period.

Dissecting this phenomenon is not something done lightly, nor is it the goal of this humble 96-page offering. Pulitzer Prize-winning journalist David Halberstam needed nearly 750 pages to do the job, and nowhere within his latest, perhaps heaviest epic—simply and appropriately titled "The Fifties"—can readers find a discussion of what made Chevy's "Hot One" so hot, a detailed description of Virgil Exner's "100 Million Dollar Look," or any reference whatsoever to "dagmars." This much lighter publication, on the other hand, is not about McCarthyism, Cold War sabre-rattling, Marilyn Monroe's moles, or Brooklyn's Dodgers moving west. As the title you passed a few pages back might indicate, this is a book about cars, particularly the fabulous cars of the Fabulous Fifties.

Like the decade itself, who can forget all those wonderful machines, many of which have grown in nostalgic prominence right along with the times

Left
Find someone who doesn't recognize the classic Chevy triumvirate, and you're probably not on this planet. Called the "Hot One" for its newfound overhead-valve V-8 performance, the 1955 Chevrolet Bel Air (front)

helped change the way buyers in the low-priced field looked at daily transportation. Chevy's Hot One grew even hotter in 1956 (middle), thanks to an optional 225hp V-8, then became everyone's nostalgic favorite in 1957 (back).

Detroit's first major styling change of the postwar era involved dumping the ever-present pontoon fenders common to all cars of the thirties and forties. Ford's all-new postwar look, introduced in 1949, was easily the cleanest of the fresh "slabside" style. That same modern bodyshell returned for 1950 (shown here) with few changes, then reappeared again in similar fashion for 1951.

from which they sprang? Some, such as modern cult favorites like the 1957 Chevy and 1957 Thunderbird, are easily recalled with enthusiasm by even the most casual observer. Others, like Studebaker's 1953 "Loewy coupe," the 1954 Hudson Hornet, and custom-bodied Buick Skylarks of 1953–1954, are far less renowned among the armchair set but are still deserving of every bit as much respect as their more publicized contemporaries. The fifties represented a veritable cornucopia of automotive delights—and disappointments. What other decade offered such disparate creations as the lavish Cadillac Eldorado Brougham and the impish Crosley Hot Shot? Classics, milestones, failures, and flops, they

SEE THE SCENERY THROUGH THE ROOF—see traffic lights easily—yet tinted transparent top protects against heat, wind, glare.

Presenting The Sun Valley—America's First Transparent-Top Car

You've seen pictures of dream cars of tomorrow. But you couldn't buy them. Now, Mercury presents America's first transparent top car to be put into regular production!

The entire front half of the roof is tinted Plexiglas. You have a wonderful sensation of driving with no top at all—but with the wind and weather protection of a sedan.

And with the great new 161-horsepower Mercury V-8 engine that makes any driving easy—the unique Sun Valley is bound to be 1954's most exciting car. See it today!

MERCURY DIVISION · FORD MOTOR COMPANY

NEW 1954

MERCURY

A new kind of power that makes *any* driving easy

were all present and accounted for in spades during the fifties.

Why? Various reasons, certainly, but the most prominent one involves the plain fact that this country's so-called "baby boom" wasn't the only explosion heard during the fifties. While U.S. military men fresh from World War II's battle fronts busily populated suburban America by doing their duty at home, Yankee industry was experiencing a growth cycle of its own, both upward and outward. Lessons learned during the war's frenzied production days were not lost as peacetime practices resumed, and it was undoubtedly the auto industry that gained the most from its education. After turning out tanks, planes, and guns at astronomical rates, supplying civilian transportation for Mainstreet U.S.A. was a piece of cake—at least as far as quantity was concerned.

By 1946, new-car-starved Americans were beating down Detroit's doors, but all Detroit could do at first was roll out a steady supply of prewar rehashes. New only by label, 1946 cars looked an awful lot like the last models built before wartime restrictions shut down automotive production early in

See-through plastic roof sections were nothing new in 1954; exotic showcars had appeared in previous years sporting transparent tops. But only Ford Motor Company tried the practice in regular production. Both Mercury's

Sun Valley and Ford's Skyliner featured tinted plexiglass instead of steel over the front seat. Mercury tried the trick one more time in 1955; Ford built its Skyliner into 1956.

Above
In 1993, Chevrolet celebrated four decades of building "America's only sports car" by rolling out a fortieth anniversary model (right), offered in one shade only, Ruby Red Metallic. When introduced in 1953, Chevy's fiberglass two-seater also came in only one shade, Polo White, and was powered by a six-cylinder engine backed by a Powerglide automatic transmission.

Right
Chevrolet's Corvette was entering its third year when Ford responded with a four-wheel legend of its own, the Thunderbird. Similar in size and also seating only two, the 1955 Thunderbird was a bird of a very different feather, offering buyers both class and comfort. Dearborn called this new style "personal luxury." After returning in 1956 and 1957, the T-bird became a little less personal when two more seats were added for 1958.

IMPERIAL

THIS MAN COULDN'T HAVE DONE BETTER . . . AND HE KNOWS IT!

He steps to the curb, dynamic and confident. He's a man who seems big, although after he has driven away you don't especially remember whether he was or not.

What you do remember is the strength of his personality, the way people went out of their way to speak to him. And the glances of approval he got when his car arrived.

It could only be one car – an Imperial. The car and the man are perfect complements – the man of substance and the most impressive car on the road today.

Imperial bespeaks power, leadership and good taste. It is designed for the man who is successful and doesn't have to prove it . . . for the man who doesn't seek prestige because he already has it.

Looking at an Imperial, riding in it, driving it . . . these things change your concept of fine car ownership. But you need more than money. Genuine good taste is a part of the purchase price. This is why the trend today, among the most critical and the most discriminating motorists in America, is definitely to Imperial.

Why not ask your Chrysler dealer for an appointment? He'll be glad to arrange one at your convenience.

THE FINEST CAR AMERICA HAS YET PRODUCED

Chrysler Corporation set off the Imperial models as a separate line beginning in 1955, the year stylist Virgil Exner put all Chrysler's divisions on Detroit's cutting edge as far as looks were concerned. One of the fifties true classics, the 1955 Imperial was easily spotted thanks to its "gunsight" taillights.

Cadillac's Eldorado Brougham of 1957 was more a palace on wheels than a car. Along with every known type of power accessory, Eldorado Brougham features also included perfume bottles, cigarette dispensers, and a mini-bar in the glove box. Throw in a stainless-steel roof, four-wheel air suspension and a 300hp 365ci V-8 fed by twin four-barrel carburetors and it was little wonder this luxury showboat cost $13,000.

1942. Promises of all-new postwar automobiles had been plentiful as World War II wound down, but since initial peacetime demand easily outstripped supply, Detroit's most prominent movers and shakers were able to take what some witnesses perceived as their own sweet time fulfilling those promises.

As a newcomer starting from scratch, Kaiser-Frazer couldn't help being Detroit's first automaker to offer totally fresh postwar cars, introduced in October 1946 as 1947 models. Another independent, Studebaker, also jumped on the totally new bandwagon in 1947. The South Bend, Indiana, automaker's flexibility came not from newness (Studebaker had been in the transportation business for nearly 100 years) but from its relative small size compared to Detroit's giants.

Gadgetry abounded in the fifties, especially from Chrysler, which offered swivel bucket seats, clocks in steering wheel hubs, and pushbutton transmissions. These buttons control Chrysler's excellent three-speed Torqueflite automatic in a 1957 300C convertible, one of the fifties most powerful cruisers.

Further proving that independents had to try harder than the heavily entrenched "Big Three," Hudson was next out with a thoroughly modern postwar model, featuring its innovative "step-down" unit-body chassis for 1948. Featuring widely spaced perimeter frame rails, Hudson's intriguing stepdown design meant the passenger compartment floor could be placed low between those rails, which in turn made for a lower, sleeker bodyshell. And like those eye-catching Kaisers and Frazers of 1947, the new 1948 Hudson featured full "slabside," modern styling—no more archaic pontoon fenders.

Among Detroit's ruling triumvirate—General Motors, Ford Motor Company, and Chrysler Corporation—it was GM that jumped out of the postwar starting blocks first, introducing a restyled Cadillac in 1948. Revamped Buicks, Oldsmobiles, Pontiacs, and Chevrolets followed in 1949, a watershed year for the modern postwar market as Ford and Chrysler also entered the fray. By 1950, the redesigned line-up was complete, and the games began.

Even though it had introduced the same basic platform in 1949, Ford greeted customers the following year with the slogan "50 ways new for 1950." If you were skeptical, you could count all 50 ways spread out right there across two pages in *Life* magazine. New, newer, newest—just when you'd thought you'd seen it all, along came another automaker's claim to top everything that had come before. Competitive pressures to build the biggest, best, most beautiful cars grew exponentially as the decade progressed, leading to rapid, welcomed, technological development, as well as some not-so-welcome design extremes. But either way, forward or backward, the American auto industry's

Chrysler Corporation, thanks to stylist Virgil Exner's touch, was head and shoulders above the rest in the tailfin department. By 1959, few cars could match the towering fins on Chryslers, DeSotos, Plymouths, and Dodges. But if there was one car that was the king of the fin era, it was the 1959 Cadillac.

progress during the fifties was anything but dull.

In 1950, Ford was still dedicated to its antiquated, valve-in-block "flathead" V-8, Chrysler Corporation was experimenting with various "semi-automatic" transmissions that shifted on their own at speed but still required a clutch for starting, and Cadillac taillights were topped by humble bulges modeled after the twin tailfins of Lockheed's P-38 Lightning fighter plane. By 1959, modern, high-revving overhead-valve V-8s had all but vanquished the old, clunky flatheads; Chrysler's bulletproof three-speed Torqueflite automatic represented state-of-the-art transmission fare; and Cadillac tailfins were boldly soaring to heights few tailfins had ever achieved.

In 1950, it seemed most cars were green, beige, or black, with maybe a red or yellow one thrown in now and again to spice things up for the truly adventurous car buyer. Five years later, a solid crimson finish was almost ho-hum in comparison to the seemingly countless two-tone combinations available. Packard and Studebaker even offered triple-tone paint schemes. And if that wasn't enough, GM customers in 1958 were left wondering if chrome had become an exterior color choice.

In 1950, Dodge, Plymouth, and DeSoto models featured what was known as three-box styling—stacked high in the middle, short, squat, and squared off at both ends—in Chrysler Corporation's best conservative tradition. Nine years later, Pontiac was leading GM towards a totally different design horizon with its long and low 1959 "Wide Track" models, cars that were illegal in some states that specified maximum body widths.

A scant four years earlier, Pontiac had begun a transformation from a stuffy, stoic company that sold cars grandpa drove to builders of true excitement. Corporate cousin Chevrolet had led the way, making a seemingly overnight transformation in 1955 by superseding its old, reliable "Stovebolt six" image with modern overhead-valve V-8 power. Simply labeled the "Hot One," the redesigned 1955 Chevy with its optional 265ci overhead-valve (ohv) V-8 almost single-handedly changed the way Americans looked at their daily transportation. A triple-digit top end had never come this cheap, and actually hadn't come much at all before GM started spreading its proven engineering wealth around to its less prestigious divisions. Once reserved only for high-brow Cadillac and Oldsmobile buyers, truly hot, high-winding OHV V-8 performance made an instant impact in the low-priced field. Muscle for the masses? You betcha. Just like that, Detroit had itself a horsepower race.

Competition of another color helped homogenize the American automaking scene as the fifties rolled on. Not that the composition of the Big Three was ever in any flux, but by 1959 GM, Ford, and Chrysler officials had next to no one to worry about other than themselves. Most independent rivals had all but fallen by the wayside, basically because they didn't have the cash to keep up with their rapidly retooling rivals.

Kaiser was a promising prospect in the years immediately following World War II, but it left the American market in 1955, taking Willys with it. Once proud, independent, pillars of the prewar automaking community, Packard and Studebaker merged in 1954 to pool their shrinking resources, then slowly faded away in the sixties. Another 1954 merger brought old stalwarts Hudson and Nash together under the American Motors banner.

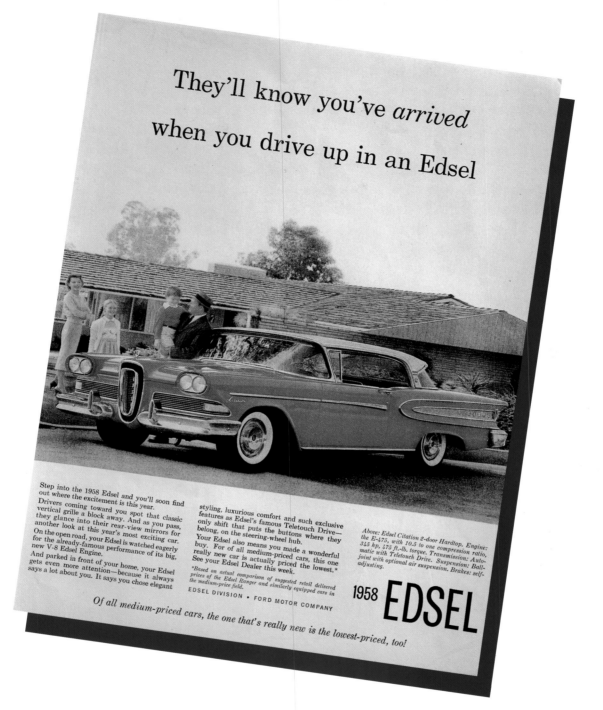

They'll know you've *arrived* when you drive up in an Edsel

Step into the 1958 Edsel and you'll soon find out where the excitement is this year. Drivers coming toward you spot that classic vertical grille a block away. And as you pass, they glance into their rear-view mirrors for another look at this year's most exciting car.

On the open road, your Edsel is watched eagerly for the already-famous performance of its big, new V-8 Edsel Engine.

And parked in front of your home, your Edsel gets even more attention—because it always says a lot about you. It says you chose elegant styling, luxurious comfort and such exclusive features as Edsel's famous Teletouch Drive—only shift that puts the buttons where they belong, on the steering-wheel hub.

Your Edsel also means you made a wonderful buy. For of all medium-priced cars, this one really new car is actually priced the lowest.*

See your Edsel Dealer this week.

*Based on actual comparison of suggested retail delivered prices of the Edsel Ranger and similarly equipped cars in the medium-price field.

EDSEL DIVISION • FORD MOTOR COMPANY

Above: Edsel Citation 2-door Hardtop. Engine: the E-475, with 10.5 to one compression ratio, 345 hp, 475 ft.-lb. torque. Transmission: Automatic with Teletouch Drive. Suspension: Ball-joint with optional air suspension. Brakes: self-adjusting.

1958 **EDSEL**

Of all medium-priced cars, the one that's really new is the lowest-priced, too!

Even though it sold reasonably well in a recession-racked year, Ford Motor Company's Edsel became the butt of countless jokes shortly after its 1958 debut. Falling well short of Dearborn's sales goal for its new mid-priced division, Edsel returned in 1959, then made one last feeble appearance the following year before exiting stage right.

In 1958, the Rambler marque supplanted the Hudson and Nash names, and the corporation managed to survive the fifties by joining the newly formed compact car ranks.

While independent automakers were struggling for their very survival in the fifties, Detroit's entrenched powers were busy overwhelming their customers with a wide array of futuristic features, clever convenience options, and dazzling design tricks. Automakers in the fifties were no strangers to gadgetry and gizmos. Headlights automatically dimmed when oncoming lights appeared, transparent speedometers mounted atop dashboards illuminated thanks to sunlight shining in through the windshield, and convertible tops went up by themselves with the first drop of rain on a fender. Ford offered a car with a tan-through plexiglass top and another that was both a hardtop and a convertible at the same time. Pushbutton transmissions, swivel bucket seats, "spinner" hubcaps, "signal tower" taillights—the list of head-turning, eye-catching, imagination-expanding, widgets and wonderments is almost endless.

Many features taken for granted just a half a decade later first appeared in the fifties. Originally, an extremely high-priced, somewhat complicated doodad, air conditioning began appearing on various options lists midway through the fifties, while four-barrel carburetors quickly became the only way to fly in the performance field.

New concepts introduced in the fifties also included an honest-to-goodness Yankee entry into the European-dominated sports car field and an all-American four-wheel ideal known as "personal luxury." The former, Chevrolet's fabled Corvette, was first on the scene in 1953 and helped inspire

the latter, Ford's lovable two-seat Thunderbird, two years later. If only Detroit could create such timeless automotive legends so easily today.

But of course not everything that rolled off a production line in the fifties was the stuff of legends. Quality control was not always up to snuff, especially early in the decade, and many models—too many actually—were certified rust magnets. At the opposite end of the decade, Detroit's move into the truly large-car field may have been inspired by the times but ended up proving that bigger isn't always better. Consequently, buyers also began to understand what "less is more" actually meant as fins skyrocketed and more and more chrome was piled on. Without a doubt, 1958 represented chrome-plating's blinding zenith, while tailfins hit their peak in 1959 before being unceremoniously clipped the following year.

Nineteen-fifty-eight also marked the debut of the one car that has come to symbolize—unjustly or not—much of what was wrong with fifties American automobiles. A victim of both a national recession as well as changing attitudes concerning styling, Ford Motor Company's Edsel quickly became the butt of jokes that are still heard today, though biting attack has long since been replaced with nostalgic amusement.

Time certainly does tend to heal all wounds, and such has been the case as far as the fifties are concerned. Most bad memories—an unpopular police action in Korea, segregation in the South, stifled sexuality everywhere (except maybe in Hollywood)—have generally been swept under the rug. Sure, there was much, much more to the fifties story than poodle skirts and ducktails, but we'll let Mr. Halberstam handle those chapters.

Even Chevrolet head stylist Claire MacKichan later admitted his men stepped a bit too far beyond sensibilities when they redesigned the Chevy for 1959. Had those flat fins stood up in typical fashion, they would have topped even corporate cousin Cadillac's high-flying appendages. Combined with a very busy grille and chrome-encrusted front end, the 1959 Chevrolet's "Manta Ray stern," as *Mechanix Illustrated's* Tom McCahill called it, inspired rival designers to describe the car as a "Martian Ground Chariot."

As far as many baby boomers today are concerned, the fifties represented a simpler time when rock 'n roll was king, Ward Cleaver was the mother of all fathers, and there was nothing cooler than an Olds Rocket 88. It was a time when kids actually pedaled around proudly with Mickey Mantle's rookie card clothespinned to their bicycle spokes, an entire family could easily afford an afternoon trip to the ballpark to see their favorite team play (on grass), and Duesenbergs were occasionally found on used car lots. And as long as nostalgia remains a great American pastime, the fifties—like Elvis himself—will never die, especially with all these wonderful reminders rolling around to keep the memories alive.

Chapter 1

Sign Posts and Mile Markers

History Makers; Good, Bad Or Ugly

Telling the tale of this country's great cars of the fifties is not something easily done in a quick read, considering everything that happened during the decade. So much history, so few years. Ten to be exact. But if you compare 1950 to 1959, it might well have been a hundred. Anyway you looked at it, from a technological perspective or with an eye towards tastes and trendiness, the transformation of the American automobile during the fifties had a lot in common with the progression of night into day.

With so much to talk about, good or bad, where do you begin? Although technology's march through the fifties cannot be overlooked, if you chose to start at the beginning, there's one major automotive attraction that rapidly grew in promi-nence right along with the years—style. No, style wasn't invented in the fifties, nor were earlier decades devoid of it. But beginning just before 1950, Detroit seemingly suddenly learned that heavy doses of style appeared to be just what the doctor ordered to keep the competition away. Whether style meant the way a car looked, or how sporty it felt, or how many gadgets it carried didn't matter. Style was style, and the fifties were soon full of it.

Before World War II, so many cars looked an awful lot like so many others. Basic transportation was the priority, with four-wheeled style and status existing only for the lucky few. After the war, car-makers quickly learned what it took to turn heads, and practical durability wasn't the answer.

Left
Seemingly overshadowed by its thoroughly modern running mates among General Motors early-fifties lineup, Buick stuck with its tried and true straight-eight powerplant while Cadillac and Oldsmobile were impressing buyers with overhead-valve V-8s. Buick styling, however, was, in keeping with fifties trends, never dull, as this 1951 Special's "waterfall" grill and ever-present "ventiports" (portholes to the casual observer) on the fender attest.

Help yourself to the open road and as far as the eye can see in any direction! Ford's new Victoria gives you the "wide-openness" of a convertible —and the comfort of a trim sedan!

Take your pick of a wide variety of smart solid or two-tone body colors! And the Victoria's "Luxury Lounge" interior features long-wearing Craftcord-leather-vinyl upholstery combinations, luxurious modern trim and a new "Safety-Glow" Control Panel —all keyed to outside colors!

You've got the world by the wheel in the

'51 FORD VICTORIA!

Relax as you ride! Ford's Automatic Ride Control smooths out the bumps before they can reach you. The Automatic Posture Control front seat insures the most comfortable driving position. What's more, you have the assurance of Ford's Luxury Lifeguard Body with a solid steel top, and Ford's rigid double-drop box-section frame with five husky cross members!

You're set for the years ahead— with 43 "Look Ahead" features from Key-Turn Starting to extra-big "Tell-Tale" Rear Lights and "Double-Seal" King-Size Brakes! See the '51 Ford Victoria—"Test Drive" it—today at your Ford Dealer's.

You get power to match the "let's go" look of the Ford Victoria—the famous 100-h.p. V-8 engine and your pick of Conventional Drive, Overdrive* or the new Fordomatic Drive*. With any of them, Ford's Automatic Mileage Maker delivers high-compression performance on regular gasoline!

You can pay more but you can't buy better!

*Overdrive, Fordomatic Drive and white sidewall tires (if available) optional at extra cost. Equipment, accessories and trim subject to change without notice.

Although Ford's 1951 Victoria hardtop kept pace with one of Detroit's hottest styling trends—the pillarless coupe design—it was still powered by Dearborn's aging "flathead" V-8, first offered in 1932. Ford's first modern overhead-valve V-8, the so-called "Y-block," didn't arrive until 1954.

An all-new, modern look was the key to luring buyers hungry for truly modern cars into showrooms. Pontoon fenders—the antiquated calling cards of the thirties and forties—were out, smooth, "slabside" bodies were in. Newcomer Kaiser-Frazer stepped out first with slabside styling in late 1946, followed almost immediately by Studebaker, Cadillac in 1948, and Ford in 1949. While GM cars and Studebakers still carried vestiges of the old pontoon style (in the rear) into the fifties, Ford's styling crew held nothing back, resulting in probably the cleanest of the early slabside designs, a look that carried over from 1950 to 1951.

While bodysides were being transformed into solid walls of steel, various dress-up tactics were also developing at the tail. Under the direction of styling guru Harley Earl, GM's designers had in 1948 added two small fins above the Cadillac's taillights, kicking off what is easily the best-known fifties styling craze. Soon all of Detroit was playing with fins, noticeable or not. Fins first sprouted on Fords in 1952, but were always relatively downplayed, while Chrysler Corporation's took off in 1957, soaring to all-new heights by 1959. Thunderbird fins in 1957 were canted, Kaiser-Willys' fins faced the wrong way, and Chevrolet tried horizontal ones in 1959. Without a doubt, the best remembered fins of the fifties were those of the 1959 Cadillac, suitably so since it was the marque that started it all in the first place.

Another stylish trend that flourished in the fifties involved the newly developed hardtop bodystyle, or convertible coupe as it was sometimes known. Chrysler had toyed with the idea in 1947, creating an attractive, airy roofline by simply attaching a steel hardtop to a Town & Country

While Chevrolet always seems to hog all the credit for being the star of the 1955 model year, the new Fords that year were certainly no slouches. Flagship of Dearborn's 1955 model lines was the Crown Victoria, the creative product of designer L. David Ash. A "Crown Vic" was easily recognized by the forward-raked chrome band that wrapped over the roof. Ford tried this trick again in 1956.

convertible body, effectively deleting the "B-pillar," or "post" common to more mundane sedans. Only seven Chrysler prototypes were built, leaving credit for actually producing a regular-production hardtop to Cadillac, which it did in 1949, rolling out the Coupe DeVille.

Typically, rival variations on the hardtop theme quickly followed. Chrysler tried it again, this time successfully, with the Town & Country in 1950, followed by Ford's Victoria in 1951, Packard that same year, and Lincoln and Mercury in 1952. Frazer even offered an intriguing four-door hardtop in 1951, although it wasn't a full hardtop in the true sense in that this somewhat peculiar Manhattan model still incorporated an odd framed window in the area where a sedan's B-pillar would have resided. More conventional four-door hardtops would soon appear from the

Always seemingly one step behind Chevrolet in the fifties, Ford also put on a new face in 1955, although history has tended to overlook that fact. Two-tone paint schemes—pleasing, contrasting, or outright clashing—came into their own that year as most automakers began offering long lists of multiple color combinations.

Big Three, and four-door hardtop station wagons would eventually come along as well, first from American Motors in 1956, then from Buick, Oldsmobile, and Mercury the following year.

Always seemingly leading the way in one fashion or another, GM also established yet another styling trend in the fifties, this one involving the windshield. Advances in glass production technology, permitted a more stylish wraparound windshield, first tried by Cadillac on its 1953 Motorama dream car, the Eldorado convertible. Unlike conventional, basically flat windshields, GM's wraparound front glass did just that; it wrapped around at the corners, making for a more open, airy feel up front, much like the hardtop roofline had done at the sides. There was a trade-off, however. Warping the windshield around the corners created a "dogleg," an obtrusive projection at the top of the door opening's leading edge required to mount the wrapped glass' frame. Many a driver in the fifties would quickly learn what those doglegs did to your knees if you weren't careful while entering or exiting, and this bruising problem wouldn't be completely solved until the sixties.

Before 1955, Chevrolets were yeoman machines powered by frugal six-cylinders carrying equally frugal price tags. Although typically dull, they were still Detroit's perennial sales leader. But Chevrolet upset the low-priced field completely in 1955 with the legendary "Hot One," a car with an all-new look as well as Chevy's first modern OHV V-8.

Also incorporating wraparound front glass was Oldsmobile's lavish Fiesta convertible, another 1953 Motorama showcar that, like the Eldorado, rolled right off the show circuit into limited production. Two other high-profile, custom-built, topless automobiles, Buick's Skylark and Chevrolet's fiberglass-bodied Corvette made the same jump that year from dream stage to reality.

Beyond the various styling tricks that came and went during the fifties, the decade also hosted

250 HP Chrysler New Yorker Deluxe St. Regis in Navajo Orange and Desert Sand

ANNOUNCING America's most smartly different car

CHRYSLER FOR 1955
WITH THE NEW 100-MILLION-DOLLAR LOOK

Everything about this dazzling Chrysler is completely new and dramatically different. It brings you a totally new fashion in modern motor car design.

The new Chrysler is inches lower in its sweeping silhouette . . . washed free of clutter . . . purposeful as an arrow shot from a bow. Its sleek new 100-Million-Dollar Look will make you feel like a hundred million dollars the instant you step inside!

And in performance this magnificent new Chrysler stands above all others. All

Chryslers are now V-8 powered with engines up to 250 HP . . . with Power-Flite, the only fully-automatic no-clutch drive that works without jerking or "time lag" . . . with the added safety of Power Brakes and the feather-light control of Chrysler Full-time coaxial Power Steering.

No other car on the road can offer you such an exciting sense of personal power and personal pride. Visit your Chrysler dealer today and see why now, more than ever before, the power of leadership is yours in a Chrysler.

to more than a few total image transformations. Most prominent perhaps was Chrysler's in 1955. Thanks to styling wizard Virgil Exner and his "Forward Look," all of the corporation's divisions benefited greatly from a complete makeover that year. From Chrysler's all-new "100 Million Dollar Look," right on down through DeSoto, Dodge, and Plymouth, the weakest of Detroit's Big Three took a big shot at reversing its fortunes by taking on a thoroughly modern image.

Gaining the most was Plymouth, a low-priced player that just one year before was boring buyers to death with its plain practicality. Under Exner's direction, Plymouth stylist Maury Baldwin created an award-winning restyle, which, when combined with the division's first overhead-valve V-8, helped bring many a customer back from the dead. Although commonly overlooked due to Chevrolet's similar rebirth that year, Plymouth's 1955 resurgence represented one of the greatest turnarounds of the decade in a year ripe with seemingly magical recoveries.

Nineteen-fifty-five may well represent the greatest turning point in modern American automotive history. Along with Chrysler's about-

Above
Even though Chrysler engineers had first equipped their cars with one of Detroit's top power sources, the fabled "hemi-head" V-8, in 1951, dull styling and a boring image slowed down sales considerably as the fifties progressed. But all of the corporation's divisions received astonishing face lifts in 1955, and Chrysler wasn't ashamed of bragging about just how much it spent on its all-new models—they didn't call it the "100 Million Dollar Look" for nothing.

Right
When introduced in 1954, Mercury's "glass-top" Sun Valley was based on the Monterey line and came in only two semi-off-the-wall colors, pale yellow or mint green. A new flagship, the Montclair, became the new base for Mercury's second-edition Sun Valley in 1955, when buyers could chose from any paint scheme offered. Only 1,787 Montclair Sun Valleys were built.

Left

All Chrysler's divisions featured new faces in 1955 as DeSoto, Dodge, and Plymouth rode the coattails of Virgil Exner's "100 Million Dollar Look." In the lesser lines, the new style was known as the "Forward Look," an image boldly demonstrated by this 1955 Dodge Royal hardtop, a marked departure from its 1954 forerunner. Complementing the fresh restyle in this case is a set of dealer-installed wire wheels.

Life magazine called it "the birth of a mechanical miracle . . . the most exciting idea in automobile design since Ford presented the first two-door sedan in 1915." "It" was Ford's 1957 Skyliner "Retractable" hardtop, a car that could be transformed from a full-fledged coupe into a convertible at the flick of a switch, a process that involved ten power relays, ten limit switches, eight circuit breakers, four lock motors, three drive motors and 610 feet of wire. Ford offered the intriguing Retractables up through 1959. This example wears a non-standard paint scheme based on Ford's original Retractable prototype.

face, Chevrolet made its legendary move into the modern market by, like Plymouth, combining an all-new OHV V-8 with stunning new styling, both features coming most unexpectedly in the low-priced field. At the other end of the scale, independent luxury marque Packard also rolled out a totally new body and its first OHV V-8, along with an innovative chassis featuring torsion bar suspension. OHV V-8 power debuted as well under the hoods of 1955 Pontiacs, which would follow corporate cousin Chevrolet towards a more youthful market. As for Ford, 1955 was the year Dearborn introduced a concept known as personal luxury in the form of the classic two-seat Thunderbird.

The back half of the decade was marked by a new trend towards longer, lower, wider looks, an

Like Chevrolet's 1957 Bel Air, Ford's early Thunderbirds are easily recognized today by even the most casual observers. Truncated two-seat renditions of Ford's mainline 1955 and 1956 models, the T-bird grew slightly in 1957 thanks to a longer tail section wearing more pronounced fins.

image first—and probably best—embodied by Exner's 1957 Chrysler products. Other attempts to jump on the bandwagon weren't quite as successful, as Chevrolet, Buick, Oldsmobile, and Pontiac in 1958 grew much bigger but not exactly better, while Lincolns and Mercurys went right off the scale into the gargantuan category. But even before the ink on its 1958 restyle blueprints had had a chance to dry, GM was rethinking its stance, resulting in Bunkie Knudsen's Wide Track Pontiacs of 1959.

Knudsen, GM's youngest-ever general manager when he joined Pontiac in 1956, had been steadily pushing his once-stuffy division into a new, youthful light, both from an image perspective and through actual performance. Under his

Many a wag in 1958 wagered whether or not General Motors had made chrome an exterior color choice all its own that year as dazzling brightwork dominated all GM divisions' offerings. A little less garish than Oldsmobile's 1958 models, Buick's topline Limited was still no stranger to ostentatious display, especially up front where that "Fashion-Aire Dynastar" grille featured 160 individual chrome squares, "the better to blind you with."

From an armchair perspective more than three decades down the road, DeSoto's late-fifties offerings may appear a bit too much. But considering just how wild things had become on Detroit's styling front by 1957, the DeSoto look that year was relatively sleek and understated. Even with those sky-high fins, overall lines were light and flowing, and bodysides were clean and uncluttered. Compared to GM cars of 1957 and 1958, Chrysler Corporation's 1957 look was certainly easier on the eyes.

direction, Pontiac's design crew took Exner's long, low, and wide ideal and gave it an unmistakable identity. Wide Track wasn't just a name, it was the way in which the all-new 1959 Pontiacs dominated the road. Of course, GM's other divisions relied on similar platforms that year, and it wasn't long before Ford was copying the concept. But Pontiac was the progenitor. What Cadillac had done for car buyers' hopes leading into the fifties, Pontiac's Wide Tracks did similarly for customers awaiting what lay ahead in the sixties.

Between the two rolled a long parade of certified classics and milestones, cars that today stand on their own merits as automotive history makers for various reasons. In the styling category, there was Studebaker's almost timeless Starliner coupe of 1953, Chrysler's regal 1955–56 Imperial, and Lincoln's stunning Continental Mark IIs of 1956 and 1957. True ground-breakers appeared in the form of "America's only sports car," the Corvette, and the aforementioned two-seat Thunderbirds of 1955–57. And from a "market-wise" viewpoint, there will always be Chevrolet's 1955 Bel Air, the so-called "Hot One," the car that introduced performance to low-priced buyers.

Other lesser known vehicles deserve a kudo or two as well. Ford's Crestliner of 1950–51 was loaded with style thanks to its two-tone paint scheme and vinyl roof. Nash's original Rambler of 1950, to a degree, pioneered compact car production in this country and would have undoubtedly made a bigger splash in another time when small would not be a dirty word. Then there were curiosities like Mercury's 1954–55 Sun Valley,

with its green-shaded plexiglass roof section. A similar model was available from Ford through 1956. When it was dropped, its name, Skyliner, was attached to an even stranger concoction, this one featuring a fully retractable hardtop that tucked away beneath the rear deck, transforming a steel-roofed coupe into a convertible at the flick of a switch. Like the see-through roof, Ford's retractable top also faded away after three years.

Another supposedly better idea from Dearborn debuted in 1958, only to disappear within three years. A victim more of bad timing than of bungling, as is often suggested, the Edsel emerged right in the middle of a national recession. It also debuted at a time when trends were moving away from the garish, overdone treatments that had marked late-fifties styling up to that point. Today, it is certainly easy to laugh at that so-called "horse-collar" grille, but not everyone got the joke thirty-six years ago. Although it did fall far short of the 100,000 sales plateau Ford had hoped for, the 1958 Edsel did find 63,000 buyers, a respectable figure that surpassed even Chrysler division's total for the year. As an all-new model line, however, the 1958 Edsel's market performance left Ford flat, and it seems that every critic since has stood by ready to make sure Dearborn never forgets.

A cosmic payback? With so many wonderful automotive memories produced during the decade's earlier years, it seemed a bit unfair to end on such a downer. But then, that was the fifties; a little of this, a lot of that, and just enough of what makes history worth remembering.

Although Pontiac would end up with all the attention for its long and low Wide Tracks in 1959, it was stylist Virgil Exner at Chrysler Corporation who first brought the look to the forefront in 1957. As with all Chrysler's divisions, Dodge models for 1958 used the same bodyshell seen the year before with only minor trim adjustments, the most notable being a switch to quad headlights. This 1958 Dodge is a Coronet Lancer, the latter being the honorable name given all of Dodge's desirable pillarless hardtop models, four-door or two-door.

Another undeniable icon of the fifties was Cadillac's 1959 models with their enormous fins, bullet taillights, and extensive trim trickery. One of 11,130 built, this 1959 Series 62 convertible cost $5,455 thirty-five years ago, roughly a dollar and a dime per pound.

With so much attention given to Chevrolet's "Hot One," few seem to remember today that Plymouth's all-new 1955 offering was every bit as fresh and exciting. Like Chevy, Chrysler's lowest-priced models also received a modern OHV V-8 that year, along with an eye-catching restyle. Plymouth's new look was attractive enough to earn "The Most Beautiful Car of the Year" by the Society of Illustrators, the first time that society had extended an award to the automotive field in its fifty-three-year history.

Pontiac was just beginning to shake off its stuffy, stodgy image when Semon E. "Bunkie" Knudsen became its general manager in 1956. A modern OHV V-8 in 1955 had begun the turnaround; once Bunkie started moving and shaking, that transformation truly started taking shape, resulting in the trend-setting "Wide Tracks" of 1959. Expanding on the long, low, and wide ideal stylist Virgil Exner had first applied to Chrysler products in 1957, Pontiac's Wide Tracks instantly became all the rage—*Motor Trend's* editors were so impressed they bestowed the new line with their coveted "Car of the Year" award.

Ford Motor Company turned down the volume slightly on Edsel styling in 1959, but it still couldn't stop a slide for the division that had began life in 1958. After about 45,000 1959 Edsels were built, Ford feebly rolled out, however briefly, one last edition for 1960 before closing the door on a chapter Dearborn would've just as soon not written in the first place.

Chapter 2

Speed Merchants

Fifties Automakers Were No Strangers to Performance

As much as America loves to remember the fifties—the music, the clothes, the cars—some details of those supposedly happier days, believe it or not, have been nearly forgotten. From an automotive history perspective, it has become all too easy these days to believe that performance—true ground-pounding, tire-melting, motorized muscle—wasn't invented until the sixties, basically because most horsepower hounds today never look back much beyond 1964, the year Pontiac introduced its ground-breaking GTO. What a concept—alotta engine in not alotta car. As far as most definitions of the modern "muscle car" read, PMD's go-getting "Goat" was the car that, thirty-something years ago, did start it all.

American automakers, however, had been running a horsepower race long before General Motors engineers discovered the obvious truth that drop-ping their largest V-8s into their lightweight inter-mediate bodies represented the easiest, least expensive way to get from point A to B in a hurry. Granted, performance developments in the mid-sixties did overshadow essentially everything that came before, but that didn't mean car buyers in the fifties were strangers to speed. Quickness, respon-siveness, road handling, and stopping power; now that was another story. Learning curves, however, do have to start somewhere, and as far as power-packed automotive engineering was concerned, the early fifties was as good as place as any.

In the beginning there was pure speed. Peri-od. Performance in 1950 was measured simply and succinctly by how fast a car would go on the top end—how long it took to reach that maximum level mattered little. Of course, as any schoolboy at the time knew, the magical triple-digit barrier

Only 300 Corvettes were built in a limited production run for 1953. Chevrolet tried again in 1954 with a nearly identical model, this time offering it in black, Pennant Red, and Sportsman Blue, along with the Polo White, the sole exterior choice the previous year.

"88"

"ROCKET"!
HYDRA-MATIC!

Oldsmobile has both!

The famous high-compression
"Rocket" Engine—plus new
Oldsmobile Hydra-Matic Drive*!
Try this thrilling combination at your
nearest Oldsmobile dealer's!

Above, Oldsmobile "88" Holiday Coupé.
*Hydra-Matic Drive optional at
extra cost on all Oldsmobile models.*

A GENERAL MOTORS VALUE

OLDSMOBILE

General Motors, without a doubt, held Detroit's hottest hand as the fifties began, both from a styling and engineering standpoint. Oldsmobile, benefiting from GM engineering's development of high-compression, overhead-valve V-8s, became the car to beat on the street in 1949. With a 303ci Rocket V-8 under the hood, the moderately sized Olds 88 was a muscular performer. And while rivals were toying with "semi-automatics" or still developing a workable automatic transmission design, Oldsmobile had GM's proven Hydra-Matic Drive, Detroit's pioneer in shiftless driving. Hydra-Matic first appeared as an option for the 1940 Olds.

Before Chevrolet's high-winding 265ci OHV V-8 made its way under fiberglass hoods in 1955, this 235ci six-cylinder was the only Corvette power source. Fed by three Carter carburetors, the Blue Flame Six made 150 maximum horses at 4200rpm.

was the mark of a truly hot machine, although few automobiles actually made that grade, and those that did took their sweet time getting there.

Early performance was also purely a function of price, as power and prestige went hand in hand. Physical laws being the same in most states, big, heavy cars needed big, powerful engines to get things rolling. In 1950, they didn't come much bigger and heavier than Cadillac, nor did they come any more powerful, thanks to GM's modern 331ci OHV V-8, introduced the year

before. Among other things, overhead valves made for better breathing characteristics and allowed engineers to improve volumetric efficiency through superior combustion chamber designs. While all other automakers were still relying on antiquated "flathead" engines with their valves situated within the cylinder block, it was GM's trend-setting, high-compression OHV V-8 that opened the door to all-new levels of power and efficiency.

At 160 hp, Cadillac's OHV V-8 may have been the fifties first power king, but it was corporate cousin Oldsmobile that probably deserves credit for building, if you will, the decade's first "muscle car." Predating Pontiac's GTO by fifteen years, Oldsmobile's Rocket 88 combined GM's cutting-edge underhood technology in a lighter, more nimble, less expensive package than Cadillac offered. The Rocket 88 debuted in 1949, featured all-new "Futuramic" styling and a 303ci OHV V-8 delivering 135 very healthy horses. Sporting a then-exceptional power-to-weight ratio of roughly one horsepower for every 22.5 pounds, the Olds Rocket 88 was revered as the strongest thing running on Main Street, U.S.A in 1950. Olds Rockets also quickly became a dominant force on the fledgling

Chevrolet's Corvette wasn't this country's only fiberglass two-seater in 1954. Independent Kaiser also took a shot at the sports car market that year with its Darrin roadster, a curious machine that suffered from poor body quality, a weak powerplant (Willys' 90hp six-cylinder), and the plain fact that Kaiser at the time was all but dead in the American market. Only 435 were built.

In keeping with Kaiser's penchant for off-the-wall design, the Darrin sportster featured sliding doors that simply disappeared into the front fenders.

National Association for Stock Car Auto Racing (NASCAR) circuit, founded by Bill France on the sands of Daytona Beach, Florida, in 1947.

Various other automakers soon followed GM's lead, adopting OHV V-8 technology as the only way to keep up in what was rapidly developing into a hell-bent-for-leather horsepower race. Studebaker introduced an OHV V-8 in 1951, followed by Lincoln in 1952, and Ford and Mercury in 1954.

Among these, Lincoln's advancement was easily the most dramatic, as a fresh, resized bodyshell was combined with a revamped chassis featuring new ball-joint front suspension, resulting in a luxury cruiser that could turn heads in more ways than one, thanks in part to its 160hp 317ci V-8. Like the Olds Rocket, the 1952 Lincoln was as much at home on the track as the boulevard, a fact demonstrated in impressive fashion during Mexico's "Carrera Pan Americana,"

The 1954 Kaiser Darrin possessed two major drawbacks. Its fiberglass body tended to show ripples and crack quite easily, and its standard 90hp Willys flathead six-cylinder engine wasn't exactly up to the task of competing with Detroit's other two-seat fiberglass sports car. But daring souls who wanted more power were in luck as some of the last cars were retrofitted with big, brawny Cadillac V-8s.

the grueling 1,900-mile endurance run first held in 1950. From 1952 to 1954, specially prepared Lincolns dominated their class in the often-fatal—for both drivers and spectators alike—"Mexican Road Race," which was open to stock, factory-equipped automobiles from all over the world. A host of engineering improvements, including Lincoln's first four-barrel carburetor, helped up output in 1953 to 205 hp, five less than Cadillac.

But as far as challengers to Cadillac's early prominence atop Detroit's powerful pecking order were concerned, Chrysler had beaten 'em all out of the gates in 1951, introducing a totally different kind of overhead-valve engine. Chrysler engineers called it their "Firepower V-8," an appropriate name for a powerplant that would 15 years later evolve into the hottest muscle machine the sixties offered. Equal in both displacement (331ci) and compression (7.5:1) to Cadillac's big OHV post-war pioneer, the Firepower V-8 featured an intrigu-

Beginning in 1951, Hudson's stepdown Hornet was the king of the fledgling NASCAR stock car racing circuit, thanks both to it overall ruggedness, as well as its unbeatable, unbreakable six-cylinder powerplant. This reproduction of one of those "Fabulous Hudson Hornets" is part of the NASCAR history display in Daytona Beach's Klassix Auto Museum.

ing cylinder head design that, like overhead valves themselves, wasn't anything new on the automotive scene, but was certainly something to brag about in its latest form.

Combustion chambers were hemispherically shaped—as opposed to the typical wedge-type layout—with a centrally located spark plug and canted valves actuated by rocker arms mounted on parallel rocker shafts. Everything about the way the so-called "hemi head" worked—breathing, flame propagation, volumetric efficiency—was superior. Weight was the only drawback as the heads were quite large. High output, however, easily offset the added pounds—at 180 hp, Chrysler's Firepower V-8 became Detroit's new horsepower leader in 1951.

DeSoto introduced its 160hp "Firedome" hemi in 1952 and Dodge followed with a 140hp version one year later. Once between the fenders of the lighter Dodge models, Chrysler's formidable

Even though it was an antiquated "flathead" competing against a host of modern OHV V-8s, Hudson's impressive 308ci six-cylinder was more than capable of throwing its weight around with a vengeance. Introduced in 1953, the Twin-H power option used dual carbs to help squeeze 160 horses out of the Hudson six. This is a 1954 Twin-H power Hudson, which was upgraded to 170hp.

hemi started setting speed records almost everywhere it went, amassing 196 AAA stock car standards during Utah's Salt Flats trials at Bonneville in September 1953.

As the old gearhead adage goes, "racing improves the breed," and so it was that nearly all automakers in the fifties were busy running all-out on tracks and in time trials in attempts to prove to potential buyers just how much their cars had improved. Along with such prominent Big Three players as Dodge, Lincoln, and Oldsmobile, independent Hudson was a checkered flag regular. Beginning in 1951, Hudson passed Olds to become NASCAR's driving force as the "Fabulous Hudson Hornets" raced to victory after victory, all without the benefit of thoroughly modern overhead valves. Or a V-8.

Up through 1954, Hudson's rugged, "step-down" Hornets ruled NASCAR not by relying on all-new technology, but by making maximum use

Relying on the neo-classic bodyshell introduced in 1953, Studebaker entered the sports touring field in 1955 with its President Speedster. Sure, the optional tri-tone paint and the huge chrome bumper may have been a bit much, but the Speedster did represent an attractive package for the lively set with its engine-turned dash, full instrumentation, and simulated wire wheel covers.

of long-standing, durable equipment. The Hornet's sting came from a 308ci side-valve six-cylinder pumping out loads of steady torque, along with 145 horses. That figure jumped to 160 in 1953 when the fabled "Twin H-Power" dual-carb option was added. By 1954, the updated 170hp Twin H-

It wasn't the biggest, it wasn't the strongest, but Chevy's 265ci OHV V-8, introduced in 1955, was the first really hot powerplant in the low-priced field. With a simple, lightweight ball-stud rocker arm design borrowed from Pontiac, the 265 V-8 could rev with the best of 'em. Maximum power of 162 horsepower (with a four-barrel carburetor) came on at 4400rpm. Compression, at 8:1, was relatively high for its day.

Power Hornet was surpassed only by Lincoln and Cadillac as far as horsepower-per-cubic-inches was concerned—and the Hudson managed this feat with two less cylinders than its rivals.

Hudson wasn't the only company in the fifties to compete without a V-8. GM's lowest priced player, Chevrolet, also had no choice but to stick with its time-honored straight six when styling mogul Harley Earl and engineering chief Ed Cole decided to introduce this country's first true sports car.

Chevrolet's Corvette was one of four GM Motorama showcars that literally rolled off a rotating stage in 1953 right into regular production. Powered by a triple-carbureted 235ci "Blue Flame" six, the little two-seat Corvette rushed from rest to 60mph in roughly 11sec, a laudable feat at the time.

Cole's engineering team trimmed more than two seconds from that figure in 1955 by installing Chevrolet's new 265ci OHV V-8, pumped up to 195hp, into the Corvette equation. And things really started heating up once Zora Arkus-Duntov got his hands on the car. A revised chassis, riding beneath a restyled fiberglass shell, appeared in 1956 along with a twin-carb 265 V-8 rated at 225 hp. Adding the optional, race-only "Duntov cam" pushed maximum output to an unofficial 240 horses. Big news, however, came the following year when fuel injection debuted atop the Corvette's enlarged 283ci small-block V-8. In maximum tune, the so-called "fuelie" 283 produced 283hp—one horsepower per cubic inch. Calling the 283hp 283 "an absolute jewel," *Road & Track* reported a startling 5.7sec 0-60mph pass for the 1957 fuelie Corvette—quick performance even by today's standards.

Attempts to rival Chevrolet's Corvette never quite made the cut. Most memorable was another fiberglass-bodied two-seater, the Kaiser Darrin,

While Chevrolet was turning heads in 1955 with its totally new overhead-valve V-8, Dodge was impressing buyers a few steps up the price ladder with its powerful "hemi-head" V-8, a division trademark since 1953. At the top of the heap, Dodge's optional Super Red Ram V-8 featured a Carter four-barrel carburetor, dual exhausts, and 7.6:1 compression. Output was 193hp. Chrysler Corporation's hemi V-8s easily dominated Detroit's horsepower race in the fifties.

By 1957, Chevrolet was offering a wide range of power levels in its V-8 passenger cars, beginning at 185 hp, produced by Chevy's two-barrel 283ci small-block. The top carbureted option was the 270hp 283 with its twin four-barrels. But for the buyer who truly wanted it all, there was the fuel-injected 283 transplanted from the Corvette. Two versions were offered, a 250hp version with 9.5:1 compression and a 283hp screamer with 10.5:1 pistons.

built briefly in 1954. Even if hadn't been hindered by its underpowered, 90hp Willys six-cylinder powerplant, this stylish, Dutch Darrin-designed sportster would've undoubtedly been doomed by its lame duck status—by the time the Kaiser Darrin made it to market, the parent company was all but finished on the American scene. Only 435 Darrins—each featuring those unforgettable sliding doors—were built before Kaiser-Willys left the U.S. in 1955 for South America.

Fellow independent Studebaker also briefly offered a sporty model, although it wasn't exactly a direct competitor for the Corvette. Studebaker had hoped to build a two-seat convertible, but after that plan failed, the reasonably sexy President Speedster hardtop was rolled out in 1955.

Chevrolet's Rochester-supplied Ramjet fuel injection system was originally the work of engineer John Dolza, who first produced a working unit in 1955. Once chief engineer Ed Cole put Zora Arkus-Duntov on the project in 1956, things really started cooking. Fuel injection was offered as the top Corvette power option from 1957 to 1965. Passenger cars were built with the optional Ramjet 283s as well in 1957, with a few also so equipped in 1958 and 1959.

Simulated wire wheel covers, foglamps and tritone paint dressed up the outside, while full instrumentation—including an 8000rpm tachometer—in an engine-turned dash were part of the deal inside. Power came from a 185hp 259ci V-8, with either a three-speed manual or automatic transmission available. Zero to 60mph times were recorded in less than 10sec and top end was about 110 mph. Not bad at all, but the Speedster still couldn't avert oblivion. Like the Kaiser Darrin, it too was a one-year wonder, leaving the Corvette to continue as "America's only sports car," a once-shaky claim that basically became a stone-cold reality by the end of the decade.

But another claim made by Chevrolet hype masters concerning their fantastic plastic two-seater wasn't true at all, although many reporters today still erroneously repeat it as fact. As much as Chevy fans would like to think that the 1957 Corvette's fuel-injected small-block was Detroit's first powerplant to reach the supposedly magical one-horsepower-per-cubic-inch level, it wasn't. That honor actually belongs to Chrysler's "beautiful brute," the 300 letter-series models. One year before Chevrolet introduced its Rochester fuel injection equipment, Chrysler customers could've equipped their 300B

Above

Ford Motor Company fans who thought the 1952-1954 Lincolns were hot luxury bombs had another coming once Chrysler introduced its letter-series models in 1955. With a 300hp hemi-head V-8 beneath the hood, the lavish 1955 C-300 emerged as Detroit's most powerful production car, and could easily run with anything on the road. An exciting restyle in 1957 fit the equally exciting 300C to a tee.

Right

Following the C-300's 300hp 331ci hemi was an even more powerful 354ci version for the 300B in 1956. Top optional power for the 300B was 355 hp, making Chrysler's luxury cruiser Detroit's first car to offer more than one horsepower per cubic inch. In 1957, the 392ci hemi (shown here) pumped out 375 horses in standard form. For $500 more, additional compression (10:1) and a high-lift cam upped the 300C's output ante to 390 hp.

Chevrolet's push into the performance field beginning in 1955 left Ford little choice but to follow. In 1957, Dearborn began offering a racing-inspired dual-carb 312ci Y-block for both its standard line and Thunderbird models. That, however, was by no means the end of it. This 1957 Fairlane is equipped with the rare supercharged 312, an option that, along with Ford's twin four-barrels, was quickly deleted once the Automobile Manufacturers Association stepped in to cut factory ties to racing early in 1957.

Identified by its E-code, Ford's dual-carb 312 produced 270hp in 1957, while this F-code Y-block pumped out 300hp with the help of a McCulloch centrifugal supercharger supplied by Paxton. A special NASCAR racing kit reportedly upped the F-code 312's output to 340hp.

hardtops with an optional 354ci hemi V-8 rated at 355 horsepower—even by today's math it isn't too tough to determine that that measures out to a tad more than one pony per cube.

Chrysler's 300 letter cars, appropriately enough, drew their name from the original model's horsepower rating—in 1955, the C-300 became Detroit's first 300hp automobile. Supplying all that power was the already proven 331ci hemi, this one featuring twin four-barrel carburetors, 8.5:1 compression and a serious solid-lifter cam. A beast beneath the hood, the C-300 was a beauty every-

where else with an attractive Imperial "egg-crate" grille up front and a standard leather interior inside. Raw performance didn't come any classier in the fifties. Nor in the sixties or seventies for that matter.

Following the 1955 C-300 came the 300B in 1956, 300C in 1957, and so on. As mentioned, the 331 hemi grew to 354ci for the 300B (standard 354 hemi output was 340hp), then jumped to 392 cubes in 1957, and finally to a whopping 413ci beneath the 1959 300E's long, long hood. Top optional output for the 300 in the fifties was 390 horses in both 1957 and 1958. No other

After the one-year wonder President Speedster came and went in 1955, Studebaker entered the sporting market again in 1956, introducing the Golden Hawk, a reasonably attractive package powered by Packard's muscular 275hp 352ci V-8. But all that cast-iron power up front also meant much unwanted weight, a plain fact that didn't help promote the Golden Hawk as a sports car. Enter the 1957 Golden Hawk with a 289ci Studebaker V-8 in place of the big Packard powerplant. To make up for the decrease in cubic inches, engineers planted a McCulloch supercharger atop the "Sweepstakes" V-8 as standard equipment for the Golden Hawk, which, like the Speedster before it, also featured a sporty engine-turned dash and full Stewart-Warner instrumentation. Supercharged Golden Hawks were built for both 1957 and 1958.

fifties-era Detroit automaker even came close to that power level.

Then again, all that muscle didn't come cheap—the gut-wrenching 300 letter cars were not only not for the faint of heart, they weren't for the faint of wallet, either. But if you preferred hemi performance without all that high-priced luxury, there was Dodge's D500 models, introduced in 1956. Aimed at sanctioned competition, Dodge's first D500 option included a potent 260hp 315ci hemi in a polite package that didn't exactly turn heads at the club like its 300 cousins, but could certainly twist a few off trackside on the NASCAR circuit. Various levels of D500 and Super D500 performance were offered each year up through the end of the decade.

The same year Dodge debuted the D500, DeSoto and Plymouth also introduced a pair of hot offerings, each heavily loaded with exclusive imagery along with ample performance. DeSoto's 1956 Adventurer was adorned with a contrasting eggshell white and gold finish, while power was supplied by a 320hp 341 hemi. Even at roughly 3,800lb, the Adventurer was a solid screamer, reportedly going from 0 to 60mph in about 10sec. Although its exclusivity diminished slightly the fol-

At 275 hp, Studebaker's blown 289 V-8 was as powerful as the Packard V-8 it replaced, yet weighed in at 100lb less, meaning the 1957 Golden Hawk handled much better than its 1956 forerunner. Maximum boost supplied by the belt-driven Jet Stream supercharger was 5psi. To compensate for that added intake pressure, compression in the Golden Hawk's V-8 was dropped from the standard 289's 8.3:1 to 7.8:1.

lowing year, the high-powered Adventurer continued as DeSoto's flagship into the sixties.

Plymouth's Fury was also a limited-edition, high-profile performer initially only offered in one shade, again eggshell white with gold accents. But in Plymouth's case, a hemi was not available; in its place was what was known as a "polyhead" V-8, an engine named for its polyspherical-shaped combustion chambers. Exclusive to the 1956 Fury was a 240hp 303ci poly-head powerplant. Much lighter than its gold-and-white DeSoto counterpart, Plymouth's Fury could hit 60mph from rest in 9sec. And unlike the Adventurer, the Fury remained an exclusive, one-finish-only offering up through 1958. In 1959, the once-coveted Fury nameplate was downgraded to yeoman duty among an entire model line, while the Sport Fury became Plymouth's top image machine.

By 1958, Chevrolet's passenger car line had grown considerably, while the fabled Corvette was easily the hottest thing rolling out of Detroit. To get those big Impalas moving, engineers turned to the new "W-head" 348ci Turbo-Thrust V-8, the forerunner to the famed 409. Maximum Corvette power in 1958 came from a fuel-injected 283ci small-block rated at 290 horsepower in top tune.

Discounting exclusive imagery, throwing aside all that extra-curricular equipment that only added to a car's bottom line, the hottest performance news of the fifties was without a doubt "The Hot One." Chevy's all-new 1955 Bel Air with its equally new optional OHV V-8 may not have been the most powerful, or even the fastest car of its day, but it was the most affordable performance machine available. Before Chevrolet's high-winding 265ci V-8 hit the scene, buyers in the low-priced field could only watch as wealthier customers hogged all the high-powered fun. And the first modern V-8 Chevy was only the beginning.

In 1956, Chevrolet passed some of the Corvette's power onto the passenger car ranks as the dual-carb 265 became an option, helping inspire *Mechanix Illustrated's* Tom McCahill to call the 1956 Chevy the "best performance buy in the world." "Chevrolet has come up with a poor man's answer to a hot Ferrari," continued McCahill. "Here's an engine that can wind up tighter than the E string on an East Laplander's mandolin—well beyond 6000 rpm—without

Introduced in 1956, Dodge's potent D500 engine option was offered with an eye towards NASCAR competition, but the package nonetheless appeared on everything from mundane four-doors to sexy convertibles. This exceptionally rare 1957 Coronet D500 convertible is one of about 3,000 D500s built from 1956 to 1961. With a 285hp 325ci D500 V-8, a 1957 Dodge could do 0–60mph in 8.5sec, according to *Sports Car Illustrated*.

blowing up like a pigeon egg in shotgun barrel." Optional fuel injection made the 1957 Chevy even hotter as maximum power reached 283 hp.

Chevrolet's corporate cousin Pontiac also turned to fuel injection in 1957 for their limited-edition Bonneville convertible. Featuring a 310hp 347ci fuel injected powerplant, the Bonneville droptop was intended as a high-profile announcement to the American market that Pontiac was no longer an old man's car company. Along with the big, brawny Bonneville, Pontiac also offered an intriguing induction option in 1957 known as "Tri Power," a triple-carburetor setup that was similar to Oldsmobile's legendary J2 equipment.

Exotic induction pieces were relatively common in the fifties. Along with Chevrolet and Chrysler, Packard, Cadillac, and Ford offered dual four-barrels, the latter fitted to both Dearborn's passenger cars and its two-seat Thunderbird for a brief time in 1957 before the Automobile Manufacturers Association's so-called "ban" on factory racing support. The AMA edict also shot down Ford's optional supercharged 312 Y-block, an engine that would've landed the high-flying T-bird right alongside Chevrolet's Corvette. Centrifugal supercharging was also tried by, of all automakers, Kaiser (in 1954 and 1955), as well as Studebaker in its Golden Hawk of 1957 and '58.

Plymouth built its limited-edition Fury from 1956 to 1958, each year preserving the exclusive image by offering the car with only one exterior appearance package. Eggshell White was the sole paint scheme in 1956; in 1957 and 1958 it was Buckskin Beige.

Either way, all three Fury hardtops were adorned with loads of gold trim, inside and out. Beneath the hood of this 1958 Fury is a gold-painted "Dual Fury V-800" V-8, a high-performance 318ci dual-carb engine that produced 295hp.

Triple carburetion appeared again among GM ranks in 1958 when Chevrolet introduced its 348ci "W-head" V-8, a bigger, more powerful engine to motivate a bigger, bulkier Chevy. The 348, forerunner of Chevrolet's fabled 409, had begun life as a truck powerplant, then developed into an honest-to-goodness performance option for a model line that was no longer based on a lithe, relatively compact bodyshell as it had been prior to 1958.

But by the late fifties, the bigger-is-better ideal had come to dominate Detroit's thinking. While nearly all cars grew in both size and weight so too did engine displacements and power outputs. As the decade came to a close, 400ci was not out of the ordinary and the 400hp barrier was just waiting to be broken. Clearly, much performance groundwork had been laid, leaving it up to a new generation of sixties movers and shakers to grab the baton and pick up the pace. That they did.

While DeSoto's first Adventurer in 1956 featured an exclusive gold-trimmed look like Plymouth's Fury, color choices were expanded for models to follow. The last high-powered, limited-edition Adventurer was built in 1959, the year DeSoto introduced optional swivel bucket seats. This 1959 Adventurer coupe, one of 590 built (ninety-seven convertibles were also produced), is powered by a 350hp 383ci V-8 fed by twin Carter four-barrel carburetors.

With its distinctive valve covers resembling a "W," Chevrolet's so-called "W-head" 348 Turbo-Thrust V-8 debuted in 1958 to help keep Chevy's bigger, heavier models in step with the times. Mounting one four-barrel carburetor in standard form, the first 348 produced 250 horsepower. Adding the three Rochester two-barrels shown here pushed output up to 280 hp.

Chapter 3

Declaration of Independents

One Step Beyond the Big Three

Decisions, decisions. These days, the seemingly endless list of automotive marques, both foreign and domestic, awaiting new car buyers in this country can, and often does, boggle the mind. Whether you're looking for an affordable compact, all-purpose utility vehicle, high-powered sportster, or loaded luxo-mobile, the choices are as plentiful as they've ever been during most of our lifetimes. It wasn't all that long ago we had it relatively easy come new model time. As late as the seventies, other than those pesky imports and maybe a lightly regarded American Motors machine or two, it was basically the Big Three or nothing at all.

Of course there are still some among us who can remember a distant time when you needed the proverbial scorecard to tell the various American automotive players apart. Although cut down considerably by the Great War that was supposed to end all wars, the U.S. automaker line-up of the twenties still made today's far-flung four-wheeled empire look like small potatoes in comparison. So many cars, so little time. Names like Auburn, Apperson, Chalmers, Cord, Duesenberg, Graham-Paige, Marmon, Moon, Peerless, Pierce-Arrow, Stutz, Westcott, Winton—and these were but a few of the more popular makes. Many, many other lesser nameplates were also present and accounted for, however briefly.

Then along came a melting pot of sorts called

Although Kaiser hype-masters preferred to promote their 1953 Dragon as a hardtop, it was obviously a four-door sedan. Helping evoke the hardtop "mirage" was a standard vinyl roof that created a continuous delineation above the side windows. The typical post was still there, but who would notice, right? A trim option introduced in 1951, the Dragon image became a model all its own for 1953. Introduced on Halloween 1952, the Dragon featured a heavy dose of what Kaiser liked to call "Bambu" vinyl. Along with the roof, Bambu vinyl also covered various interior panels, the package shelf, seat trim, and dash, and even was found in the trunk and glove box. Wire wheels were optional, while 13-karat gold-plated trim was standard 1953 Dragon fare.

the Great Depression, a national economic disaster that claimed many once-great carmakers along with countless other businesses. By the time another global war arose to wake up the American economy, Detroit's automaking giants, General Motors, Ford, and Chrysler, were solidly entrenched as the "Big Three," while all other surviving rivals were simply "independents." Like the Big Three, those independents strong enough to ride out the Depression years were all treated to a piece of the defense contract pie during World War II. And as peace neared, President Franklin D. Roosevelt made it clear that the wealth would remain spread around after the war, proclaiming that any and all independent automakers would be given every chance within his wide powers to compete with the big boys.

Prominent proof of what F.D.R. had in mind before his death in April 1945 quickly appeared in the form of the Kaiser-Frazer Corporation, a newborn independent incorporated in August that year. Founded by former Graham-Paige Motors Corporation president Joe Frazer and powerful ship builder Henry Kaiser, Kaiser-Frazer joined this country's automaking fraternity in a big way, setting up shop in the huge Willow Run facility outside Detroit, courtesy of a Reconstruction Finance Corporation lease. One of the world's largest buildings at the time, the Willow Run plant had been constructed by Ford Motor

White sidewall tires and wheel discs available on all models at extra cost

Presenting the "next look" in cars

NEW 1950 STUDEBAKER

Success breeds success! The car that led in modern design now moves still more spectacularly out ahead!

The new 1950 Studebaker is here—and you can see at a glance that it's America's "next look" in cars.

Here's the dramatic and unexpected sequel to the tremendously popular "new look" in cars that Studebaker originated three years ago.

Here's a truly inspired 1950 Studebaker—dynamically new in form and substance—America's most advanced new car—styled ahead and engineered ahead for years to come.

Paced by a breath-taking new Studebaker Champion in the low-price field, this is a complete line of completely new 1950 Studebakers.

Each one is increased in wheelbase length and over all length—thrill-packed with the new performance of higher compression power—comfort-cushioned with self-stabilizing new Studebaker coil springs.

Discriminating America is giving the 1950 Studebaker an enthusiastic welcome. Stop in at a nearby Studebaker showroom the first chance you have. See the 1950 Studebaker—the "next look" in cars!

©1949, The Studebaker Corporation, South Bend 27, Indiana, U. S. A.

Studebaker was more than happy to tell the world in 1947 that it was the "first by far with a postwar car." Three years later, after nearly all other automakers had left South Bend in the dust, Studebaker began barking again after rolling out another new car. But while the company's first modern postwar models had brought buyers running by the proverbial droves, the next step up the ladder into 1950 left many witnesses scratching their heads. "Which way is it going?" was one of the more popular comments.

Henry J styling was interesting to say the least, especially for a low-priced budget machine. This 1953 Corsair rolls on non-stock, owner-installed modern tires. Total Henry J production in 1953 was 16,672; only 1,123 the following year.

Company in 1940 to manufacture bombers for the war effort. Moving into Willow Run certainly represented a coup of sorts for Henry Kaiser and Joe Frazer, but it was just one of many rapid, major steps towards what appeared as a very promising future, at least from a late-forties perspective. Time, however, would soon tell the true tale.

After beating the Big Three out of the postwar blocks with an all-new, modern model, this one featuring stunning slabside styling, K-F jumped to the top of the independent heap in 1947, outselling even established Studebaker, Nash, Hudson, and Packard. But as the fifties dawned, Kaiser-Frazer was already on a downhill slide, due to a malady already well known among the independent crowd—the bucks simply weren't big

General Motors wasn't the only automaker in 1953 to roll a dream car image right off the stage onto the street. Packard's sexy 1953 Caribbean convertible was a direct descendant of designer Richard Arbib's 1952 Packard Pan American show car. Unable to channel the body like Arbib did, Packard stylist Dick Teague nonetheless added a nice array of personal touches to the Caribbean to help set it apart from the standard line. Included was a hood with a functional scoop, fully rounded rear wheelwells and a continental spare tire in back. Dazzling wire wheels also helped add to the distinctive look. Only 750 Caribbean convertibles were built in 1953, followed by 400 in 1954. An all-new body and tri-tone paint arrived for the Caribbean in 1955, when 500 models were sold. Production of the final rendition in 1956 was 276 convertibles, 263 coupes.

enough to allow continued competition with the much wealthier automaking powers. After selling 144,507 cars in 1947, K-F sales peaked at 181,316 the following year, rallied briefly at 146,911 in 1950, then dropped steadily; 99,343 in 1951, 75,292 in 1952, and 21,686 in 1953. Frazer, the higher-priced of the two parallel model lines, disappeared entirely after 1951, leaving Kaiser to struggle on alone, albeit briefly.

As early as 1951, Henry Kaiser had begun talks with Willys-Overland chief Ward Canaday concerning the purchase of Canaday's firm, which had been in and out of operation through various partner- and directorships in Toledo, Ohio, dating back to 1907. Probably best known for its hard-working "Jeeps," Willys kicked off the postwar era by also offering utilitarian station wagons, then introduced the practical, playful Jeepster in 1948.

Willys re-entered the passenger-car market in 1952, rolling out its innovative "Aero" line, very attractive, easy-to-handle little cars that were at the same time reasonably roomy and politely compact.

In the summer of 1953, Kaiser bought Willys, with all Kaiser-Willys production eventually relocating to Toledo as the coveted Willow Run facility was sold to GM. It was, however, the beginning of the end, at least as far as American customers were concerned. Not even a pooling of resources could prevent the inevitable, and Kaiser-Willys pulled up stakes in 1955 then moved to Argentina.

Although it was a short stay in the U.S. market for Kaiser it certainly wasn't uneventful. Intriguing offerings included a four-door hardtop, a four-door convertible, and what may well be considered this country's first hatchback, the Traveller. Innovative models also included the compact Henry J, introduced in 1951, and the sleek 1954 Darrin two-seater, America's other fiberglass sports car. And as far as looks were con-

Nash may well have copped honors for the most alarming all-new postwar design when it introduced its Airflyte line in 1949. Like the later Edsel, these "bathtub" Nash models have since found a place in countless comedic skits, but innovative aspects of the aerodynamic Airflyte was nothing to laugh at; it was easily the most efficient shape produced in the early fifties, if not the entire decade. And if cutting-edge aerodynamics weren't your cup of tea, there was also Nash's little Rambler, a car that debuted in 1950 as Detroit's first relatively successful compact. Nash even went so far as to offer a convertible Rambler, which could drop its top but had to leave the window frames and rails in place.

Before Nash had debuted its compact Rambler in 1950, Powel Crosley, Jr. was this country's main small-thinking automaker, and to this day his cars easily rank right down there with the smallest ever built in America. In back to the left is a 1951 Crosley sedan. Crosley also built station wagons and open sports cars before discontinuing production early in 1952. The yellow curiosity in front is a 1950 Skorpion, a custom-bodied Crosley featuring a fiberglass roadster shell originally marketed by the Wilro Corporation of Pasadena, California. On the right stands one of Crosley's competitors, the "mail-order" King Midget, a kit car produced in Athens, Ohio, from 1947 to 1970. This red 1958 King Midget is one of 5,000 sold during the company's twenty-three year run.

Small cars were one thing, but small utility vehicles? Introduced in August 1950, Crosley's diminutive Farm-O-Road was "designed to do big jobs on small farms—or smaller jobs on big farms." Optional Farm-O-Road equipment included a pickup bed with or without a hydraulic dump mechanism, front and rear power take-offs, and a hydraulic drawbar in back for mounting various implements. Among the latter were a 10-inch plow, rake, spike and disc harrows, planter, seeder, cultivator, and two mowers, a standard unit and a large, three-gang commercial affair. Later in 1959, Crofton Marine Engineering, in San Diego, California, brought Crosley's Farm-O-Road back to life, producing identical models called the Crofton Bug and Brawny Bug.

cerned, Kaiser-Frazer didn't take a back seat to anyone.

Even with a limited budget relative to the Big Three, K-F did manage to stay close to Detroit styling's cutting edge, thanks to, among others, veteran designer Howard "Dutch" Darrin, of pre-war Packard fame. If onlookers thought the first

Kaisers and Frazers were attractive, they had another thing coming once a Darrin-inspired restyle appeared in 1951. Problem was, that body, like the one that had debuted late in 1946, had to last far too long for its own good. Once buyers became bored with the look, the Kaiser was just another car left in the dust by the Big

The 1951 Frazer 4-door Sedan shows the clean, new beauty of the spear-motif design. Its wondrously low price makes the Frazer the fine-car buy of '51!

The 1951 Frazer Vagabond—the famous 2-cars-in-1—converts in 10 seconds from luxurious 6-passenger sedan to spacious carrier...for sports or business equipment!

five new handcrafted body styles 1951 FRAZER

Truly built to better the best on the road, the 1951 Frazers are handcrafted—with regally rich interiors in a wide variety of exclusive colors and fabrics. All models are powered with the new Supersonic High-Torque Engine. Hydra-Matic Drive, optional at extra cost.

The Pride of Willow Run

The 1951 Frazer Convertible America's only 4-door convertible has added convenience, comfort, spaciousness and visibility...of course a fully automatic top!

The 1951 Frazer Manhattan comes in *two* models—one with its metal top coated in glamorous colors, the other with its top covered in shimmering nylon. Either way enhances to the utmost the convertible look in solid steel.

© 1950 KAISER-FRAZER SALES CORP.

Three. Among other things, Kaiser never did overcome the lack of a modern OHV V-8, a stumbling block that didn't trip up Studebaker.

Self-proclaimed as the "first by far with a postwar car," Studebaker had followed up its all-new 1947 model with an even more alarming restyle in 1950, a look that left many critics without a straight face. Wags continually asked which way the "bullet-nose" 1950 Studebaker was going, a reaction to the coupe's wraparound rear glass that seemingly echoed the pointed nature of the car's front end. Kibitzers, however, stopped laughing in 1951 when Studebaker debuted a modern OHV V-8, quite an achievement for the independent automaker that had begun life building farm wagons in South Bend, Indiana, nearly 100 years before.

Like Kaiser, Studebaker relied on high-profile styling in an attempt to lure buyers away from the Big Three fold. Although Raymond Loewy often receives sole credit for Studebaker's trendy appearance, it was young stylists under Loewy's direction like Virgil Exner (before he went on to bigger and better things at Chrysler) and Robert Bourke who actually did the bulk of the pencil work. That work included the neo-classic 1953 Starliner hardtop, as clean and sleek

Like Nash, Kaiser-Frazer was no stranger to innovative design. After plans to offer a front-wheel-drive car fell through, Joe Frazer and Henry Kaiser set their sights a bit lower and still managed to amaze many onlookers with their models' creativeness. Intriguing offerings, shown here in this 1951 Frazer ad, included a four-door hardtop, Detroit's only four-door convertible at the time (which, like the Rambler, went topless with its window

rails still in place), and the industry's first hatchback. Kaiser also offered a hatchback, the Traveler, and a similar four-door hardtop, the Virginian. But all this creativeness aside, nothing could change the realities of competition, and cash-strapped Frazer didn't survive much longer than it took for the ink on this advertisement to dry.

In 1947, Studebaker had emerged as one of this country's first automakers with a truly new postwar car. But by 1950, the newness had worn off, leaving the South Bend, Indiana, independent no choice but to go back to the drawing board. Stylist Robert Bourke of

Raymond Loewy's design studio supplied a facelift for 1950. Front or rear, the 1950 Studebaker easily represented a love it or hate it proposition. *Earl Davis photo*

a look as any automaker, established or independent, unveiled in the fifties.

But as much as Bourke's beautiful bodyshell—sometimes called the "Loewy coupe"—was worthy of praise in 1953, it, like the Kaiser restyle of 1951, ended up being over-used as it reappeared in slightly dressed-up form each succeeding year. Being an independent, Studebaker was not immune to the aforementioned cash-crunch malady. Retooling expenses simply proved too great. Whereas GM, Ford, and Chrysler could afford to spend tens of millions of dollars on a new model every three or four years, their various rivals couldn't. And also like

Kaiser, Studebaker officials soon found themselves looking for strength in numbers.

In June 1954, Studebaker's Harold Vance and Paul Hoffman met with Packard's James Nance to announce the latter independent automaker's purchase of the 102-year-old South Bend firm. Once-proud Packard, a Detroit pioneer and builder of high-line automobiles that had been, just twenty-some years before, rivaling the classic Duesenbergs as the finest machines this country could offer, found itself outclassed in the fifties as Cadillac, then Lincoln sped away with all-new looks and updated engineering.

As if the 1950 Studebaker's pointed "spinner" nose didn't attract enough attention—both positive and negative—the wraparound rear glass helped inspire many a wag to ask, "which way is it going?"
Earl Davis photo

Packard was the first independent to offer a modern automatic transmission—Ultramatic—in 1949, but its 1950 "bathtub" body remained tied to pre-war tastes, and its antiquated straight-eight L-head was out-and-out old news. Restyled sheet metal in 1951, followed again by another modern remake in 1955—this one riding atop an all-new torsion-bar chassis mounting an equally new, powerful OHV V-8—couldn't make up for lost time. Or respect. After selling 104,5937 luxury models in 1949, Packard sales fluctuated mildly, then dropped like a rock to 27,307 in 1954.

Nance needed someone to help him pay the intimidating bill for the 1955 model's total transformation, thus the deal with Studebaker, itself a company in dire need of some extra cash. As it turned out, the Studebaker purchase only succeeded in dragging Packard down to its death; in July 1956, the Curtiss-Wright Corporation took over troubled Studebaker-Packard, Nance resigned soon after, and Packard operations in Detroit ceased in August. Even though the Studebaker-Packard corporate name carried on into the sixties, the last Packards—glorified Studebakers wearing different trim and badges, as they had since 1957—rolled off the South Bend line in July 1958.

Hudson saved the best for last as far as its excellent stepdown chassis models were concerned. Introduced in 1948, the stepdown Hudsons lasted up through 1954 before Hudson was transformed into "Hash" after the company's merger with Nash. Perhaps one of the mid-fifties most attractive models, the 1954 Hornet easily made for Detroit's sleekest four-door sedan with its long, low lines, a direct product of the stepdown design.

A bad deal on Nance's part? Actually he had originally hoped to save the day for Packard by tying the Studebaker-Packard agreement into an even bigger merger, this one to fall in line under George Mason's American Motors banner. Mason, head man at Nash-Kelvinator in Kenosha, Wisconsin, was the main mind behind the scheme, which involved uniting the major independents to maximize their strengths, all in an effort to better compete with the Big Three. The first part of his plan became official on April 22, 1954, when Nash and fellow veteran independent Hudson merged.

Under Mason's visionary direction, Nash had

One of the most coveted engineering features of the fifties was the modern overhead-valve V-8, a design that left the age-old "side-valve" flatheads in the dust. OHV V-8s truly came into their own in 1955, the year low-price rivals Chevrolet and Plymouth introduced theirs, joined by Pontiac and independent Packard. Displacing 352ci, Packard's new OHV V-8 came far too late to turn the once-proud marque's fortunes around.

become a pioneer in compact car production, introducing the little Rambler in March 1950 and the even smaller Metropolitan four years later. And although many then, and since, have laughed at Nash's total postwar restyle in 1949, the "Airflyte" line's superb aerodynamics, as well as its innovative unit-body construction, was no joke. On the other side of the coin, Hudson built typically large automobiles, but had also left the mainstream in 1948 with its rugged "stepdown" design, itself uti-lizing unitized body-frame construction. Mason's American Motors merger, however, brought an end to the stepdown Hudson as AMC production was consolidated at Nash's Kenosha works, where much of the 1955 Nash look, as well as its engineering, was transformed into a totally new Hudson, a model sometimes unflatteringly labeled a "Hash." The last stepdown left Hudson's old Jefferson Avenue factory in Detroit on October 29, 1954.

As for the second half of the American Motors

With one last lunge before his company was dragged down to death by Studebaker, James Nance vainly attempted to bring Packard into the thoroughly modern fifties in 1955, spending everything his company had (and much of what it didn't) on an attractive restyle, a new overhead-valve V-8, and an innovative chassis that featured long torsion bars in place of conventional springs for all four wheels.

plot, Mason did apparently intend to join his Hudson-Nash co-op with Studebaker-Packard once James Nance had finalized that deal, but the idea never got beyond the talking stage. Although reasons for the failure are varied, the prime stumbling block came October 8, 1954, when George Mason died of pneumonia. Mason's replacement atop American Motors, George Romney, wanted no part of yet another merger with two obviously ailing automakers. And that was that. Studebaker-Packard limped on towards eventual death in the sixties, while Romney's American Motors was born again in 1958 as the decision was made to unceremoniously dump the Nash and Hudson lines and stick only with the compact Rambler, a move that proved right in step with the times. By 1960, even the Big Three were building small cars.

In the sixties, light, agile, practical compacts would finally come into their own after literally decades of disinterest had left various automakers holding the bag following attempts to market small cars. During the fifties, few buyers even considered

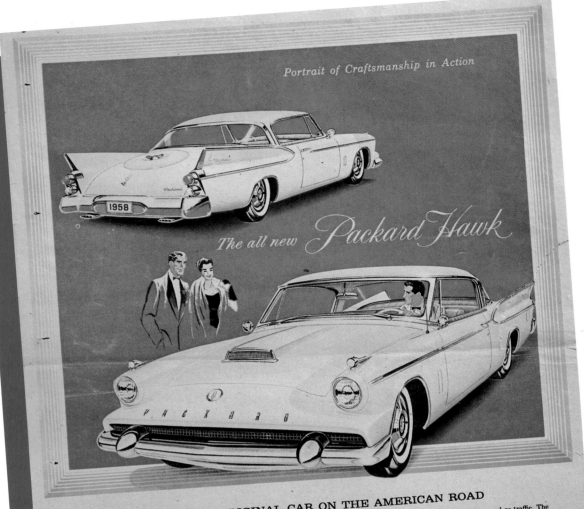

Portrait of Craftsmanship in Action

The all new *Packard Hawk*

1958

THE MOST ORIGINAL CAR ON THE AMERICAN ROAD

You will find no other car like the Packard Hawk. It is the most original and distinctive automobile crafted in America, styled to match the tempo of our times. Its unique flowing lines are aerodynamic. Its fins: functional. It is designed with that imaginative flair you only expect to find in Europe's most fashionable automobiles. Faithful to its thoroughbred breeding, the Packard Hawk is a *luxury* automobile with smooth, soft leather seats and elegant, tasteful interior appointments.

Extra Power from Built-in Supercharger

Its appearance is complemented by power from a highly efficient V-8 engine with a built-in supercharger, capable of instantaneous acceleration, or smooth performance under the most trying conditions of stop-and-go traffic. The supercharger with variable speed drive cuts in automatically as needed, for acceleration or extra power for passing or hill climbing, but when not in use, costs nothing extra in gasoline. It is a design for power, with economy.

The Packard Hawk is *the* new car with a regal air that immediately distinguishes its owner as a man of position. Put yourself in that position . . . behind the wheel of a Packard Hawk, soon.

Studebaker-Packard offers the most varied line of cars in America. See them all . . . economy cars . . . sports cars . . . station wagons . . . luxury sedans and hardtops.

Visit your Studebaker-Packard dealer today!

Studebaker-Packard
CORPORATION
Where pride of Workmanship comes first!

Above

Basically a Nash with Hudson nameplates added, the 1955 Hornet represented the beginning of the end for a once-proud independent that had ably battled its much larger Detroit rivals throughout the early fifties. One of 4,449 V-8 Hornet four-door sedans built for 1955, this model is also equipped with air conditioning, a rare, as well as high-priced option in those days.

Left

While Nash and Hudson were moving in together to form AMC, Studebaker and Packard were setting up shop under one roof in South Bend, Indiana. Sadly for the once-great luxury marque, the same thing that happened to Hudson also happened to Packard. After 1956, Packards were nothing more than rebadged Studebakers. And in the case of the odd 1957 Packard Hawk, the badge wasn't the only thing changed. Basically a Studebaker Hawk with an awful extended nose tacked on, Packard's Hawk soared only with turkeys. Luckily, South Bend officials saw fit to put the Packard nameplate to rest in 1958.

Designed by stylist Phil Wright and engineer Clyde Paton, Willys attractive Aero line debuted in 1952. Attractive both in form and function, the easy-to-handle Aero models might have met a better fate in another time and as a product of another automaker. As it was, Willys merged with troubled Kaiser in 1953, then headed south to Argentina with its parent company in 1955. This is an Aero Lark, one of six different Aero lines offered by Kaiser-Willys in 1954.

small cars, basically because most believed what they were told—bigger was better, right? Nonetheless, more than one attempt was made to convince customers that affordable compacts were the wave of the future. As mentioned, of these efforts, Nash probably showed the greatest success, although Henry Kaiser certainly gave it one helluva try with his pint-sized Henry J of 1951–54.

But if you want to talk small cars, really small cars, they didn't come much smaller than Crosley. Refrigerator mogul, radio magnate, owner of the National League Cincinnati Reds baseball team,

Powel Crosley first offered his somewhat odd, certainly tiny "car for the forgotten man" in 1939. When Crosley's compact creations reappeared in 1946, they weighed only 1,150lb, rolled on an 80in wheelbase, and cost less than $1,000. Innovations in 1949 included four-wheel disc brakes and the so-called "COBRA" four-cylinder engine, the name coming from its copper-brazed sheet metal cylinder block. Neither the brakes nor the Cobra engine were without their bugs, but that didn't stop Crosley from continued creativeness.

That same year Crosley introduced the Hot

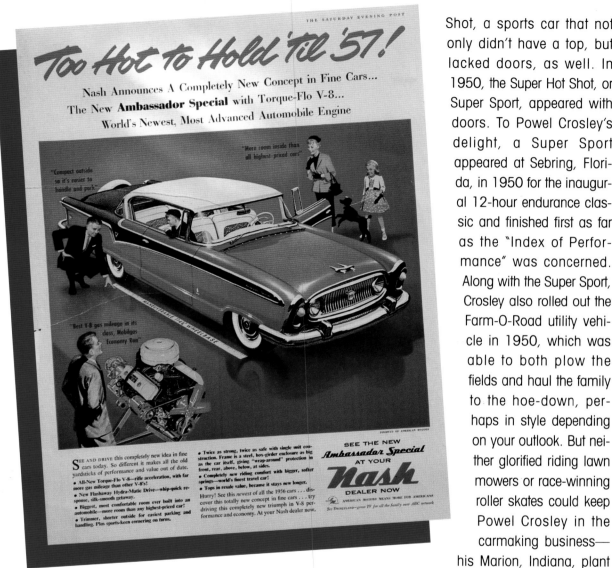

Too Hot to Hold 'til '57!

Nash Announces A Completely New Concept in Fine Cars...
The New Ambassador Special with Torque-Flo V-8...
World's Newest, Most Advanced Automobile Engine

"More room inside than all highest-priced cars"

"Compact outside so it's easier to handle and park"

"Best V-8 gas mileage in its class, Mobilgas Economy Run"

MEASURABLE FULL WHEELBASE

SEE AND DRIVE this completely new idea in fine cars today. So different it makes all the old yardsticks of performance and value out of date.

● All-New Torque-Flo V-8—rifle acceleration, with far more gas mileage than other V-8's!

● New Flashaway Hydra-Matic Drive—whip-quick response, silk-smooth getaway.

● Biggest, most comfortable room ever built into an automobile—more room than any highest-priced car!

● Trimmer, shorter outside for easiest parking and handling. Plus sports-keen cornering on turns.

● Twice as strong, twice as safe with single unit construction. Frame is a steel, box-girder enclosure as big as the car itself, giving "wrap-around" protection in front, rear, above, below, at sides.

● Completely new riding comfort with bigger, softer springs—world's finest travel car!

● Tops in resale value, because it stays new longer.

Hurry! See this *newest* of all the 1956 cars . . . discover this totally new concept in fine cars . . . try driving this completely new triumph in V-8 performance and economy. At your Nash dealer now.

PRODUCT OF AMERICAN MOTORS

SEE THE NEW
Ambassador Special
AT YOUR
Nash
DEALER NOW

AMERICAN MOTORS MEANS MORE FOR AMERICANS
See Disneyland—great TV for all the family over ABC network

Shortly before his death in 1954, George Mason merged Nash and Hudson into American Motors, a move that effectively ended Hudson's identity as the cars themselves merged with Nash in both form and function. By 1957, that form was truly something to catch the eye—for whatever reason is your call.

Shot, a sports car that not only didn't have a top, but lacked doors, as well. In 1950, the Super Hot Shot, or Super Sport, appeared with doors. To Powel Crosley's delight, a Super Sport appeared at Sebring, Florida, in 1950 for the inaugural 12-hour endurance classic and finished first as far as the "Index of Performance" was concerned. Along with the Super Sport, Crosley also rolled out the Farm-O-Road utility vehicle in 1950, which was able to both plow the fields and haul the family to the hoe-down, perhaps in style depending on your outlook. But neither glorified riding lawn mowers or race-winning roller skates could keep Powel Crosley in the carmaking business— his Marion, Indiana, plant shut down in July 1952. Luckily he knew how to sell refrigerators and radios.

Various other independents, diminutive or otherwise, came and went during the fifties; most are barely worth mentioning. As for the prominent ones, the decade represented a make-or-break proposition, a situation that couldn't have made Detroit's dug-in Big Three any happier.

Always one to step out from the crowd, Henry J. Kaiser transformed his interest in a "people's car" ideal into a sheet metal reality in 1951, then named the car after himself. The little Henry J turned many heads early on; 82,000 were sold the first year. But like the Kaiser company itself, Henry J's Henry J quickly faded from the scene then disappeared completely after 1954.

It's Here! Nash Presents a Completely New Kind of Car ...the Metropolitan!

Four years ago we presented for public opinion the prototype of an entirely new kind of car . . . an American concept of European motor car design. It was seen by hundreds of thousands of enthusiastic motorists across the nation. Their opinions have gone into the car we present today . . . the all-new Metropolitan. It is revolutionary in economy and operating costs, new in handling ease, and thoroughly American in comfort and performance. Read about it here . . . then accept our cordial invitation to see and drive the Metropolitan.

No matter what car you are driving now, you'll want to see and drive the exciting new Metropolitan. The result of 11 years' research by Nash—an entirely new kind of car, a *new size* of car for today's driving needs!

It's a *family* car . . . practical for small families, a sensible second car for large families . . . offering up to 40 miles to the gallon!

It's a *pleasure* car . . . a dashing, road-hugging *sportster* . . . exciting to drive . . . proudly styled, beautifully made . . . and handles like a sports car.

It's a *business* car, perfect for those who use a car constantly—and want *lowest* operating costs and amazing parking ease.

Come and see the finest and most luxurious car of its size ever built. A car that can ride three in front, with an extra utility seat in back.

Here's more good news! Whether you choose the Convertible or the "Hardtop" model, the low, *low* price *includes* Weather Eye Conditioned Air System, custom radio, directional signals, continental rear tire mount, foam rubber cushions with custom nylon and genuine leather upholstery. There's nothing more to buy!

Yes, the Metropolitan is *all automobile.* Built as a double-rigid structure—protecting you with unitized Nash Airflyte Construction. Built with Nash quality—Nash ruggedness—and completely bonderized for rust protection. Built like all Nash cars for a double lifetime of service.

We invite you to see and try this exciting new kind of automobile—sold and serviced by Nash dealers everywhere. Then you'll know why everybody's talking about the new Metropolitan.

SOLD AND SERVICED BY NASH DEALERS FROM COAST TO COAST

HOLIDAY/APRIL

UP TO 40 MILES A GALLON!
- Official records in 24-hour NASCAR supervised runs: Non-stop economy test—41.6 miles a gallon at 34.7 m.p.h. Performance test—1469 miles at an *average* of 61 m.p.h.
- Choice of two models—Convertible and "Hardtop"
- Powered by the famous Austin A-40 overhead valve engine
- Continental Styling on a new scale
- World's Easiest Handling and Parking
- Riding Comfort of a Large Car
- Airflyte Unitized Construction—World's strongest and safest
- Lowest of Operating Costs

Metropolitan

NEWEST MEMBER OF THE

Nash

Airflyte Family

Ambassador • Statesman • Rambler

Built with a "Double Lifetime" . . . Your Safest Investment Today . . . Your Soundest Resale Value Tomorrow

Nash-Kelvinator's George Mason tended to think small in big ways. First came the 1950 Rambler. Then in 1954, Nash introduced the truly small Metropolitan, a car perfect, in Mason's mind, for the congested byways of the rapidly growing American suburbs. In 1959, Metropolitan sales had reached an amazing 22,000 units. Nonetheless, the car was dead by 1962.

Chapter 4

Carrying The Load

Not All Memorable Machines of the Fifties Were Cars

A Almost lost among the seemingly endless roll call of unforgettable passenger cars built in the fifties is a lengthy list of notable utility vehicles; station wagons and trucks that, at the very least, helped American buyers change the way they looked at station wagons and trucks. Once relegated to the mundane workaday world, both forms of transportation experienced a transformation akin to Cinderella's on the night of the big dance as style, status, and prestige were injected into what had historically been a purely practical equation.

Station wagons had not exactly been strangers to the good life before the fifties began, as a few had been aimed at the tea and crumpet set, who often needed a hard-working second

Chevrolet's most expensive model, at $2,857, the Nomad wagon returned for its last appearance in 1957, when 6,534 were built. Pontiac also ended its two-door Safari run that year after building 1,292 1957 models. Both divisions, however, continued using the once-exclusive nameplates on conventional four-door wagons.

vehicle to, perhaps, haul the wife's tennis partners and their gear to the club. But even though some station wagons had shown up in the luxury car ranks, nearly all wagons in the early-fifties were spartan, to say the least. Most featured wood-framed bodies, a quaint if not primitive throwback to an earlier, less technologically developed time.

Indicative of just how primitive things could be in the thoroughly modern postwar era were the "woodie" wagons offered by Willys—simple, low-priced, bare-bones transportation built with cargo hauling first and foremost in mind. But while Willys was attempting to keep prices—as well as expenses—down by rolling out an essentially identical woodie wagon year after year, Detroit's big boys were tooling up for a change as the fifties dawned, trading troublesome wood for low-maintenance all-steel bodies. And not only did the new steel wagon bodies insure better quality (less rattles, more durable), they also lent themselves easily to the same styling touches applied to the passenger car lines.

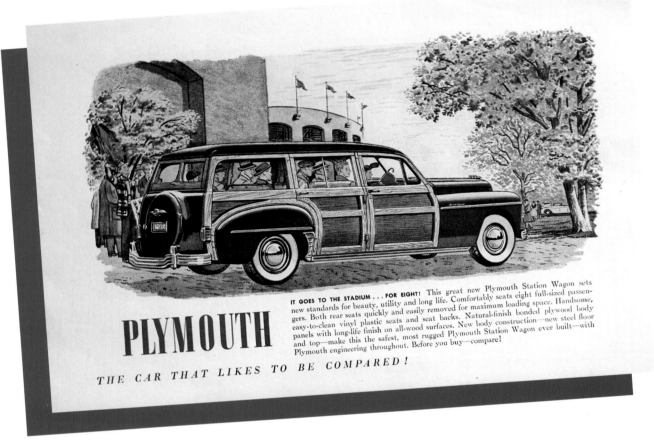

IT GOES TO THE STADIUM . . . FOR EIGHT! This great new Plymouth Station Wagon sets new standards for beauty, utility and long life. Comfortably seats eight full-sized passengers. Both rear seats quickly and easily removed for maximum loading space. Handsome, easy-to-clean vinyl plastic seats and seat backs. Natural-finish bonded plywood body panels with long-life finish on all-wood surfaces. New body construction—new steel floor and top—make this the safest, most rugged Plymouth Station Wagon ever built—with Plymouth engineering throughout. Before you buy—compare!

PLYMOUTH

THE CAR THAT LIKES TO BE COMPARED!

Before the fifties, station wagons were all "woodies," in that they used wood-framed bodies, a cheap, easy way for any and all automakers to market cargo-carrying renditions of their passenger line cars. But during the decade's early years, Detroit began dropping the wood bodies in favor of all-steel wagon construction, which didn't rot, swell, or become termite infested. Rust, however, was another story.

General Motors seemed especially endeared to classy wagon production, and by 1957 was manufacturing various four-door pillarless hardtop versions that could both catch the eye and bring home the groceries. The pillarless hardtop, an all-new postwar styling trend introduced in regular production by GM in 1949 (Chrysler had tried the trick earlier in limited numbers), did away with the typical sedan's B-pillar—the "post" that cut the side glass area into front and rear sections—resulting in an open, airy look reminiscent of a ragtop. It was no coincidence that early hardtops were labeled "convertible coupes."

Whatever the name, a two-door hardtop still looked sweet, and it didn't take long for designers to add that look to four-door models, then station

Ford's first all-steel station wagon appeared for 1952, and reappeared in nearly identical fashion up through 1954. This Sheridan Blue 1954 Customline Ranch Wagon is powered by Ford's 130hp 239ci "Y-block," Dearborn's first modern overhead-valve V-8. Notice how the license plate was designed to swivel out as the tailgate went down.

wagons. Although American Motors was the first to build a pillarless hardtop wagon—the 1956 Rambler Custom Cross Country—there was no denying that Buick's stylish Caballero and Oldsmobile's Fiesta of 1957 were about as snazzy as it got among the four-door station wagon crowd. Less dazzling but equally trendy were the various four-door hardtop wagons introduced by Mercury that year.

But easily the most stylish among the fifties wagon crowd was Chevrolet's Nomad, a sporty two-door traveler introduced in 1955. Although two-door wagons were nothing new, the Nomad was certainly a ground-breaking creation, com-bining youthful pizzazz and upscale prestige with all the purposeful utility typically offered by the yeoman family wagon. Critics with large families may have bemoaned the lack of an extra set of doors, but who really cared when the thing looked so darn good on the way to the corner store?

The work of Chevrolet styling studio head Claire MacKichan and stylist Carl Renner, the Nomad began life as one of three Corvette proto-types built for GM's 1954 Motorama show circuit. Key to the image was an attractive ribbed roof supported by light, forward-raked pillars, a design Renner penned. GM styling chief Harley Earl liked Renner's work so much, he had MacKichan apply

85

How soon they forget. Or did they? In 1953, Oldsmobile image-makers had used the Fiesta name for an exclusive, limited-edition luxury showboat, a convertible cruiser that wouldn't have been caught dead hauling the Little League team to the park. Four years later, those Olds men dusted off the nameplate for their classy four-door hardtop wagon, undoubtedly as a way to tie in the new utility model with an existing high-profile image.

the idea to Chevy's standard two-door station wagon for 1955. A regular-production version appeared in February.

Along with Renner's roofline with its wraparound side glass, the 1955 Nomad also featured exclusive bodyside spears, full rear wheel openings (passenger cars were "scalloped"), and seven vertical trim bars on the tailgate that, like the roof pillars, incorporated a distinctive forward rake. Next to nothing from the cowl back was shared with the standard wagon line. Inside, exclusive interior treatments included chrome headliner bows and special pleated upholstery with "waffled" inserts. Linoleum lined the rear cargo floor. Available with either the "Stovebolt" six-cylinder or Chevrolet's all-new 265ci OHV V-8, the Nomad wagon didn't come cheap—at roughly $2,500, a V-8-powered 1955 Nomad cost more than a Bel Air convertible.

High-priced or not, the classy Nomad returned in 1956, this time without the exclusive bodyside trim, special upholstery, and modified rear wheel openings. Even then, there was no mistaking the look, which returned one more time for 1957 before being dropped from the ranks at year's end. Chevrolet label makers opted to continue using the Nomad name—beginning in 1958 it was stuck on the more conventional four-door wagons—but it just wasn't the same.

Less renowned, yet of equal note was Pontiac's version of the Nomad, the Safari. Despite com-

While Chevrolet's first Nomad shared a front clip with the standard passenger car line, much of the design from the cowl back was exclusive to the two-door sport wagon image. Special features included radiused rear wheel openings, a ribbed roof with forward-sloping pillars, and a canted tailgate with its ribbed trim.

plaints from Chevrolet people who wanted to keep the idea to themselves, Pontiac's movers and shakers were able to wrestle Renner's roofline away from MacKichan's studio and apply it to the two-door Chieftain 860 line, which rolled on a 122in wheelbase, seven inches longer than the Nomad. That difference, however, was all part of the plan as the Safari was intended to be a bigger, better Nomad.

Pontiac's 1955 Safari came standard with the division's first OHV V-8 (287ci) backed by a Hydra-Matic automatic transmission—no six-cylinders or three-speed manuals here, although a six could be requested. Few were. Standard Safari features also included leather upholstery and carpeting in the rear cargo area. Of course, all this added up to hefty asking price, some $500 more than the V-8 Nomad's bottom line. That aspect alone was enough to limit the Safari's appeal, nonetheless Pontiac followed Chevrolet's lead and offered the high-profile model up through 1957, when declining sales finally forced the issue. Like Chevrolet, Pontiac also continued using its once-exclusive nameplate on lesser machines after the sporty two-door Safari was dropped.

Always seemingly at the cutting edge, whether it was engineering, styling, or general design,

Unlike the 1956 and 1957 Nomads, Chevrolet's 1955 model was also equipped with exclusive interior treatments including "waffled" vinyl seat inserts. This particular fully loaded 1955 Nomad wagon features optional air conditioning, a luxury that cost upwards of $500 in the mid-fifties.

General Motors was also at the lead when it came time to transform the image of the American light-duty pickup truck. Much more so than station wagons, light trucks had really never been anything but light trucks before 1955. A cargo bed, a cab, sturdy ruggedness—what else did you need to haul manure down to the lower forty? Style, comfort, and class were basically never considered by truck buyers, at least not until Chevrolet rolled out its Cameo Carrier pickup.

B.C., "Before Cameo," pickups were purposefully plain, not pretty. Although some options were offered and color choices were available, most trucks on or off the road were devoid of creature comforts and were seemingly either black or dark green. Bumpers and most grilles were painted to match the body, and trim was basically non-existent, as was convenience. Then along came Chevrolet's Cameo to stir things up.

Introduced March 25, 1955, the elegant Cameo Carrier half-ton pickup was unlike anything truck buyers had ever seen. Detroit's first high-class hauler, the Cameo combined various car-like styling cues with all the utility typically found in a truck, although a buyer probably would've thought twice about dumping a load of manure into that stylish cargo bed with its cab-wide fiberglass sides. Abundant trim, attractive custom taillights, an airy cab featuring trendy wraparound glass, and an exclusive Bombay Ivory/Cardinal Red paint scheme made the classy Cameo Carrier tough to miss, whether parked at the club or sitting at a loading dock.

And just like that, trucks were no longer meant only for the Oshkosh B'gosh crowd. A touch of style outside, a little more comfort inside, maybe an optional automatic transmission—all these attractions and more quickly became pickup selling points after Chevrolet had shown customers a truck didn't have to be all work and no play. While the Cameo carried on for four years, Chevrolet's standard truck line was becoming an attraction in itself as more options, a higher level of trim, and even two-tone paint choices were made available, all advancements not overlooked by the competition.

While Ford never went so far as to offer anything as lavish as the Cameo, it did respond in 1957 with a slightly dressier pickup known as a "Styleside." Like the Cameo, Ford's Styleside trucks featured a trendy, clean-looking, cab-wide bed in place of the age-old pontoon rear fenders found on most trucks of the day. Chevrolet retaliated with its Fleetside models in 1958, the same year the Cameo was finally discontinued.

Not to be outdone, the Dodge boys replied with a stylish pickup of their own in 1957, and they didn't just rely on car-line styling cues, they went right for the real thing. Introduced in May 1957, Dodge's so-called "Sweptside" pickup was, up front, a D100 half-ton truck, itself a restyled machine featuring hooded headlights, a new grille, and a trendy wraparound windshield (which had debuted in Dodge ranks two years before). In back, however, all bets were off as the Sweptside's cargo bed made even the Cameo's creative box pale in comparison.

While lower-priced Chevrolet and Pontiac shared the Nomad image, higher line Buick and Olds both offered stylish four-door hardtop station wagons in 1957. Buick's was the Caballero, a high-class hauler that featured "Riviera styling"—a reference to Buick's first use of the pillarless hardtop roofline—the 1950 Roadmaster Riviera coupe.

Then and now. The 1956 Ford F100 shown here is indicative of how bland pickups were during the decade's early years. Thirty-five years later, light-duty trucks were anything but dull, as this 1991 F150 XLT 4x4 demonstrates. Chevrolet first began adding true style and class to its pickups in 1955. Ford didn't respond until 1957.

Proving that you didn't always need a lot of money to turn a few heads in the car (or truck) business, Joe Berr, manager of Dodge truck's Special Equipment Group, simply had SEG employee Burt Nagos weld a pair of high-flying fins, taken off a 1957 Dodge Suburban two-door wagon, right on to the Sweptside's bed in place of those old, boring pontoons. Somewhat amazingly, the station wagon quarter panels, complete with those "signal tower taillights," fit like gloves, as

Chevrolet changed the pickup market forever in 1955 by introducing the Cameo Carrier, a stylish half-ton truck with a fiberglass bed and various car-like styling cues—notice the taillights and deluxe wheel covers. Offered only in an exclusive Bombay Ivory/Cardinal Red paint scheme, Chevy's first Cameo found 5,220 buyers. One of 1,452 Cameo's built in 1956, this polite pickup is powered by a six-cylinder—the dual exhaust system is an owner-installed feature. Additional Cameo paint choices were also added in 1956.

did the Suburban's rear bumper. Once a little extra trim was added to the cab to match the wagon's existing beltline brightwork and a somewhat crude cut-down tailgate was mounted between those sweeping fins, the job was done. Whether you liked the look or not, you couldn't knock Berr for at least trying to keep up with the Joneses.

Like its Cameo counterpart, Dodge's Sweptside was hindered by a high price and a limited market niche—stop and think, would you bang a

Yes, those are standard 1957 Dodge car quarter panels on this truck. Dodge designers created the 1957 "Sweptside" half-ton by simply welding Suburban station wagon rear sheet metal—complete with those unmistakable taillights—right onto the D100 pickup's cargo bed. A somewhat simple, cutdown tailgate, the Suburban's chrome rear bumpers, and matching trim for the cab completed the package.

toolbox over those fins? A certified novelty in 1957, the intriguing Sweptside reappeared in 1958 only to find few takers, then was quietly discontinued in January 1959. By then, Dodge's less eccentric, and certainly stylish "Sweptline" pickups had debuted to do battle with Ford's Stylesides and Chevrolet's Fleetsides. By 1960, a truck buyer was faced with a nice choice of half-ton trucks that looked good while working hard.

And if that buyer was truly adventurous, he could try out Ford's Ranchero, a curious vehicle that was half car, half truck. Both a ground-breaking attention-getter and a throwback to the prewar days when most light trucks were simply passenger car front ends followed by cargo beds, the Ranchero debuted in 1957 as "America's first work or play truck." But unlike its prewar ancestors, which were more truck than car underneath, Ford's 1957 Ranchero was very much a car, with the added convenience of a truck-type bed thrown in for good measure. Extra-cost Ranchero equipment included nearly all the comforts of home—

Although Chevrolet did offer its classy Cameo Carrier for four years, demand diminished considerably once the standard half-ton line was treated to a long line of comfort, convenience, and appearance options. This heavily loaded 1957 3100 pickup is equipped with a 283ci V-8 backed by a Hydra-Matic automatic transmission. Additional attractive features include two-tone paint (the white cab accent), various trim baubles, and deluxe wheel covers.

Ford kicked off the "car-truck" craze in 1957 with its first Ranchero, a vehicle that featured a convenient cargo bed but was far less truck than it was car. Both six-cylinder and V-8 power was available, as were an impressive list of convenience options such as power steering and brakes.

electric seats and windows, automatic transmission, power steering and brakes—while optional two-tone paint only made the package that much more attractive. Ford's 223ci "Mileage Maker" six-cylinder was standard, but a Y-block V-8 could be added for a few dollars more.

Not only did the Ranchero kick off a playful, practical legacy that continued into the sixties, it also inspired a rival counterpart from Chevrolet. Two years after Ford's "car-truck" debuted, Chevy introduced its El Camino, which was Spanish for "the road." Buyers who opted for Chevrolet's Ranchero response in 1959 found themselves hitting the hard road in style, at least as far as *Motor*

With Ford's gauntlet laid down, Chevrolet couldn't help but retaliate with a "car-truck" of its own. Introduced in 1959, Chevy's El Camino was built just one more year before being temporarily discontinued. Chevrolet would reintroduce the idea, on the all-new A-body Chevelle platform, in 1964.

Life's editors were concerned. In their words, "even the [El Camino's] cab has rakish lines—more so, one might say, than the Ranchero inasmuch as the rear window is not squared off but has a graceful forward slope." Although somewhat oversimplified, both car-trucks were essentially station wagons with the rear roofs removed. But in the El Camino's case, the chop job was done with a bit more grace compared to Ford's effort. Like the Ranchero, Chevrolet's El Camino continued on into the sixties with great success.

Ten years after it had begun, the fifties closed after bringing about change after change after change. And perhaps nowhere in the four-wheeled world were those changes more radical than among the practical transportation class, where rugged dependability and rawboned utility were reformed and fashioned into an attractive package basically taken for granted today. Comfort, convenience, cargo capacity, and class? Who woulda thunk it?

American car buyers of the fifties, that's who.

Index

Bourke, Robert, 70
Canaday, Ward, 66
Carrera Pan Americana, 43, 44
Cole, Ed, 48
Crosley, Powell Jr., 68, 78
Earl, Harley, 23, 48, 85
Exner, Virgil, 26
fins, 23
Frazer, Joe, 64
hardtop body style, 23
Kaiser, Henry, 64, 66
Knudsen, Semon E., 29, 36
Loewy, Raymond, 70
MacKichan, Claire, 85
Mason, George, 73, 75, 79
NASCAR, 43, 46
Renner, Carl, 85
Romney, George, 75
three-box styling, 16
Willow Run Plant, 64, 65
wraparound windshield, 24, 25

Vehicles
American Motors, 73, 75, 85
Buick, 21, 30
Cadillac, 14, 15, 34
Chevrolet, 12, 16, 25, 39, 58, 59, 61, 83, 85–89, 91, 93–95
Chrysler, 13, 52, 53, 55
Crosley, 68, 69, 78, 79
DeSoto, 31, 61
Dodge, 27, 33, 45, 46, 56, 59, 89, 90, 92
Ford, 10, 12, 17, 18, 22, 28, 29, 32, 37, 54, 85, 89, 90, 92, 94
Hudson, 15, 45, 47, 48, 73, 77
Kaiser-Frazer, 14, 16, 42–44, 49, 50, 63–66, 69, 70, 80
Lincoln, 43
Mercury, 26
Nash, 32, 67, 74, 81
Oldsmobile, 40, 42, 86
Packard, 28, 66, 71, 72, 75, 77
Plymouth, 26, 35, 57, 60
Pontiac, 16, 59, 86, 87
Studebaker, 14, 47, 50, 56, 64, 70–72
Willys, 66, 67, 78, 83